"THE MOF

"THE MORPHER"

A Spiritual And Surrendering
Journey Of A Woman Living To
Die With Sickle Cell Disease

Sydatu Holder

To order additional copies
Xlibris
1-888-795-4274
www.Xlibris.com
Orders@Xlibris.com
702461

To my parents Big Jim, Bettie and Ethel,
my siblings Lance, Keyatta, Nivia and James K.,
the rest of my family and friends especially my bff Aisha
whose love support, inspiration and prayers encouraged, uplifted
and sustained me during my journey up
the rough side of life's mountain.

CONTENTS

"God wrote this book! After my name (Syd) it's all God"
The author wishes to acknowledge all those persons,
angels send by God, especially the staff of Xlibris,
whose invaluable assistance helped make this dream a reality.

Having done ALL . . . STAND.

"Therefore put on the full armor of God, so that when the day of evil comes you may be able to stand your ground and after you have done everything, TO STAND."

—Ephesians 6:13–14, NIV

Art is the ability to tell the truth, especially about oneself—even when it hurts.

—Richard Pryor (1940–2005)

FOREWORD

Why Am I Writing This Book?
The "Why" Behind the "What"

MOST PEOPLE WITH serious ailments—for instance, cancer survivors—write books to elicit support and awareness or campaign for a cure. I've asked myself why many times during my emotional awakening—yes, emotional, because that is the sum word for everything in my heart that is now in this book and hopefully will be your awakening upon completion. An emotional awakening that forced me to be honest with myself about what was really going on with me and within me and what my role has been throughout, good or bad. Telling the truth about myself and what I went through with no holds barred and no bull crap, the surrendering journey that forced me to write this book.

Please don't misunderstand me; I'm not suggesting that anyone or anything forced me to write this book. I was faced with doing it when I really did not want to do it, because of my spiritual belief and values. As you will find out throughout the book, the main thing that I stand on, the main factor that grounded me and made me triumphant through this whole losing battle, through this whole journey, is my faith and trust in Jesus Christ. My firm and tireless belief that God has a good plan, a purpose for everyone, and that nothing happens by chance or accident, there's a reason for everything.

What I've gone through the entire span of my life was not for nothing. I know in my heart that God did not orchestrate my life filled with more physical, emotional, mental, and financial pain and suffering—the whole gamut, more than most people can ever imagine, let alone ever experienced themselves—for nothing.

God is love and would never let his children go through the fire "just because." No, I believe God gives each and every person who has suffered an injustice or disservice, whatever it may be—whether illness, abuse, abandonment, or harm—beauty for ashes. So standing on that "anchor," if you will, I believe God's promise to give me "a crown of beauty for ashes—for your shame you shall have double" (Isa. 61:3 and 7).

Writing this book, chronicling my journey, and opening up the eyes of people who don't know or have a clue about sickle cell anemia disease is part of his good plan for my life. Yes, that may sound well mapped out and a just cause to write a book, basically taking you back to what I said about most people who write about their journey and experiences. However, believe it or not, it was neither my aim nor my desire to write this book. You really cannot fathom how much I did not want to do this project. I mean what regular person, who doesn't know how to even go about writing and putting a book like this together, let alone take on this enormous feat as a nobody, or beyond an unknown, tackles this all on her own? I'm not a celebrity. I have no money, but I have faith and I guess a tiny bit of courage for which, once again, I certainly cannot take credit for, because from start to finish I was scared out of my mind. I have no contacts or even the ability to hire a ghostwriter or biographer to do it for me after hearing my story. I have no idea what I'm doing, and you have no idea how preposterous it is for me to be doing this. I always say God wrote this book and I can only take credit for writing my name in the typeset! After my name, it's all God.

I can't even begin to tell you how much of a fight and resistance I put up throughout the whole project, because I did not want to do it. Seriously, it's taken me the better part of *five years* to complete the doggone thing. I mean really, who takes that long to write one dang book? I would start writing, and I'd write over the course of several days, then I'd set it aside and not touch it again for several months. But the entire time I wasn't working on it, I'd have this nagging feeling in my stomach, and I'd hear over and over in my head, "You have to write and finish this book, even if you never publish it, to bring awareness and possibly help someone else going through similar experiences. Even if you never ever do anything with it except have it occupy space on your laptop, you have to write it for yourself."

It was almost a way of gaining closure within myself, to finally release all the hurt and pain that was built up inside of me. Often, instead of letting it out at the time of the painful circumstance or hurt and brokenness, I would suffer silently through. I would push it down and push it down so far beneath the surface that it was hidden even from myself. I remained silent and believed that I was okay. I could handle it. I was a soldier, but I just let it build up deep down inside. I was gorgeous and would look and act like I didn't feel awful or hate myself, which I did deep down for the longest time.

It wasn't until I started working on this project that I really started to see and feel those things that were locked inside of me, because recalling the journey uncovered and floated all that pain right to the surface. It caused me to really take an honest look at myself and put aside my pride long enough to say "This hurt me" and "That hurt me" about all those hurting things that really devastated me. I was no longer this so together, "I'm not going to let anything or anyone break me" person, which is the attitude I shouldered my entire life. I was a soldier. I could take the pain. Most times, during the few and far between instances when I did sit down to write, as the words were coming up from within me and onto the pages, I would be bawling and crying, uncontrollable sorrow escaping their hidden home within me. I was just devastated writing about hurts and pains so deeply buried that my friends, family, and everyone who knew me did not even know anything about or, much less understood.

I am not the first, and I certainly will not be the last African child of color (Negro descent) to suffer from sickle cell disease, a disease until recently had no public face. My desire is not to be some poster child for sickle cell disease. I am a voice that needs to be heard, to bring awareness and to provide a spirit and a face that others like me can identify with. I feel it is due time sickle cell had a face, upon which I offer mine.

I am an African American female who has suffered from sickle cell disease for over thirty years, my entire life. I have gone through

"THE MORPHER"

and continue to go through the physical, mental, and emotional effects of a disease for which there is, to date, no cure.

My story is one of courage, long-suffering, and triumph. So for me, it is imperative that those who suffer, who have loved ones, or know someone who suffers from sickle cell disease get a firsthand inside look at sickle cell for what it is. Hopefully, you can find understanding and enlightenment from my story. Also, my mission and my hope is that this book reaches some person regardless of age, gender, race, creed, culture, or background out there who suffers from a debilitating or life-altering illness or disease, not necessarily sickle cell disease. A person who has been told by physicians, their families, or anyone that you cannot do x, y, or z, that you will not be able to lead a normal life or have normal everyday childhood experiences and accomplishments. You will not participate in normal activities whether it is sports, extracurricular, or academic or whatever you desire to do in general because of an illness and physical limitations, "so just get used to it, accept it, and do the best you can." I am a living witness to the contrary.

From as early as I can remember, I have been told by physicians that I have an inevitably high mortality expectation, that I will not live to be this age or that, setting various ages for certain death. They told me that I would not be able to and should not even attempt to participate in normal childhood activities such as biking, swimming, tennis, basketball, or other sports, which I loved and desired very much to do. I should not participate in any activity that could cause overexertion or fatigue, and I would be limited in just about every area of normal life experiences and activities. Not only should I accept that fact but I should bow down and submit to it and get used to living this limited life they had all laid out for me.

According to them, a person with sickle cell disease to the severity of which I had it (SS—the most severe out of all the variations of the disease) did not have the physical, mental, or emotional capacity to withstand any strain or stress. In other words, forget about the quality of life and being able to do things to make you happy and allowing your spirit to soar and just do nothing in order to extend the quantity of life. Well, God gave me the gifts of stubbornness, determination, resilience, persistence, the ability to persevere, a lot of heart, an unquenchable fighting spirit, and the courage and strength to use it all—to DEFY! I am an "I will not go quietly into the night" kind of person. The more someone tells me I cannot do something, the greater my will and desire to do just that! I'm here to say I have gone through the fire. I have walked in your shoes and can tell you firsthand there DOES NOT have to be such a thing as CANNOT in your life. If you want whatever it is you desire for your life bad enough—IT IS ATTAINABLE. Having a normal life is possible! It is attainable! Take control! YOU set your own limitations because in the end, you will be the one to have to live with those same limitations that are set in place for your life.

CHAPTER 1

Overview of Sickle Cell Disease

S ICKLE CELL ANEMIA (SCA) is an inherited disease in which there is a defect in the hemoglobin.

The technical, scientific definition of sickle cell anemia (SCA) is a "severe, hereditary anemia occurring among the offspring of parents who both have the sickle cell trait or disease." An inherited disease in which there is a defect in the hemoglobin but I call it and will probably refer to it throughout the rest of this book as the Morpher. I've come to call my beloved disease the Morpher or Morph for short as such, because it causes such a metamorphosis in me, my body, and my entire overall state that I myself often do not recognize the two separate states and the radical changes the disease and its symptoms enforce. I've often felt like and identified with the Incredible Hulk animated cartoon (fictitious character) in the sense that one minute I'm the normal David Banner human version of the monster, and with the slightest change or variation, I catalyze and transform into this hideous monster. My face becomes distorted with pain; my body and limbs gnarl up as though I've been possessed by both the creatures from the television show *Tales from the Crypt* and the *Hunchback of Notre Dame* simultaneously.

It's really a scary thing! For as long as I have been experiencing this "morphing" phase that occurs with the onset of the pain from a sickle cell crisis, I still cannot get over how quickly and drastic the changes enact themselves. There've been times when I'm out having a good time, hanging out—you know, laughing, joking, and the whole lot—one minute, and in the next moment, I'll feel the unmistakable initial "twinges" of the Morph. What I call "twinges" is the initial intense spark of pain that goes torpedoing through my body, seemingly like a bullet ricocheting through every bone and joint, one right after the other, until it feels like every bone in my body is broken and has been set on fire.

It continues on like this at such a rapid pace that within a ten- or twenty-minute period, I go from being this normal, active, productive, and vibrant person, and in the next moment, I transform into this virtually paralyzed, pain-stricken, helpless, pathetic mess. I mean, I can't breathe. I can't move a single limb without excruciating pain; a lot of times I can't even speak. I'm in too much pain to even speak. Can you imagine that? If that's not definitely morphing, I don't know what is.

In all this, I must say my sympathy lies with those who are with me or around me when the sudden onset of my crisis occurs. Understandably, most people are just beside themselves, like onlookers witnessing the most horrific vehicular accident or train wreck they've ever seen. The shock written all over their faces as they stare at me is always so transparent, at least to me, because I've seen it a million times. Even those individuals trying to hide it by putting on their bravest front on my account, it's written all over their faces, and I can read them like a book. Sometimes I almost want to reach out and console them, and oftentimes, I do.

One earlier encounter comes to mind, illustrating the wear and tear that is felt by everyone involved. I was about eight years old at summer camp, going about my day as usual, when the Morph's fireworks began. It was Friday, and I anticipated just another regular, uneventful day like every other day of the two weeks I was spending at Camp Wamava in the Blue Ridge Mountains. I'd had a long week, had put in a lot of hours of various camping activities, and I was ready for a break.

I was swimming in the lake with the other kids when the Morph appeared. The Morph quickly took over my legs and arms, and I couldn't drag myself out of the lake. I must've tried at least half a dozen times before finally dragging myself out of lake. I was exhausted and thought to myself, as I struggled to get myself together and ready for the fireworks, *Oh well, here we go again, it won't be the first time.* I wasn't tripping. No point getting all stressed out over the other kids and staff looking at me like the alien at the camp in the movie *Meatballs*. Just get me some medical help, please.

Mommy, making only seven dollars an hour at that time, had to hire an ambulance to transport me from the camp all the way to Children's Hospital in Washington, DC, where I experienced the mother of all sickle cell crises. Little did I suspect that on top of all that, I was turning green from a ruptured gallbladder. I was hurriedly taken into surgery, and that was the end of camp and what was left of the summer for me. That just ticked me off! Why did God make me like this?

Don't get me wrong; it's not like I didn't appreciate all the love I was getting, but on this particular day, the Morph had once again cut into my fun time. At the rate things were going, I was never going to get out of this hospital in time for some summer fun. Not! I was getting out of there in time for summer if it killed me. Little did I know it would just about come to that. I lost not only the rest of summer but also two months of school in the fall. Why did God make me this way? I would try doing all the things other kids my age were doing—biking, swimming, gymnastics, etc.—to prove I was normal and just as good as anyone else. I would be able to for a short while, then I would get gravely ill doing those very same normal, everyday things I loved to do. Why couldn't I be normal?

CHAPTER 2

My Earliest Memory of the Disease

M Y EARLIEST MEMORIES of my illness were trips to Children's Hospital, in Washington, DC. I wasn't more than six years old, but I remember it like it was yesterday. Most of the time, my mother would have to drive me to the hospital herself because at the time, we lived so far away in Silver Spring, Maryland, and only private ambulances would travel the distance to Children's Hospital in Washington, DC. My mother wouldn't have me going to just any hospital. Children's Hospital had the best pediatric facility in the area, and that is where she wanted me to be.

I remember the forty-five-minute drives to the hospital were long and painful. It was like I could feel every pebbled rock, crack, and bump in the road. The pain would surge through my body like a sharp electric current, absorbing every movement with the slightest bounce of the car, like the shocks holding the undercarriage of the vehicle. My tiny body would go rigid and curled up in the front bucket seat of my mom's gold Datsun 310, as I tensed up and held my breath so as to try and brace myself for the surge of sharp pains. This intense pain would grip my entire body, and I would scream and wail in pain.

As time went by and I got a little older, I wouldn't cry so much. It seemed the crying only increased the pain and the misery of the whole episode, because when you cry, there is a split moment of time that you have to relax your body to exhale/inhale between sobs, and in that brief moment, you leave yourself open for the "thunderbolt," as I used to call the lightning-sharp surge of pain that comes frequently and intensely as a bolt of thunder during a violent storm. I would try hard to relax my body to induce the flow of oxygen. I hated being caught off guard when the surges came, so I would try to reserve my strength by bracing my body for the anticipated strikes of pain. Why did God make me like this? Why couldn't I be normal?

Most people feel relief when they get in sight of a hospital for needed treatment after an accident or for an illness because they're thinking, *Yes, finally, I'll receive some help, something to make me feel better.* Not me. When I'm sick and inevitably en route to the hospital, the sight of it does not bring me any comfort or joy—at least not anymore. As a matter of fact, it invokes emotions that are the exact opposite of that of relief.

A better way to explain it would be to say when I see that emergency entrance, I'm torn. Yes, a part of me way down deep is relieved. However, the majority of me, especially my body, is dreading the impending ordeal with a deep, foreboding feeling. I guess the most accurate correlation would be the feeling you get when you're on the way to the dentist to get several cavities filled. Essentially, you know that it's a necessary evil, but you also know when you get in that chair, it is almost certain that you will be made to feel worse before you feel better. That is exactly how it is. I dread the experience because I know that I'm going to go through hell and a whole lot of crap and have to talk to a lot of seemingly stupid and incompetent people (everyone seems stupid and incompetent when I am in so much pain).

Yet instead of doing things to help my pain—or at least not add to it—they continue doing things to aggravate the pain and annoy me by asking me what seems like a million questions. Questions which, at the time, seem redundant, pointless, unfruitful, and just a plain waste of time. All this in addition to experiencing an ever-increasing high level of unbearable pain—as a direct result of all the doggone moving around they make me do—as though I'm not there to be treated for a *severe pain* crisis. I mean just the diagnosis alone says it all: SEVERE PAIN. You'd think they'd get a clue, like "DUH, PEOPLE . . . ONE AND ONE EQUALS TWO, IT'S NOT ROCKET SCIENCE HERE!"

I always think, just once, I would love for these morons to be on the other side of the table or, in my case, the other end of the thermometer. Whenever I'm sitting in the emergency room in agonizing pain (the kind of pain most people have never experienced nor can imagine), watching every second tick by on the very same black-and-white wall clock that seems to adorn every hospital emergency room in the country, I need a little more urgency from the doctors and nurses instead of them floating around all nonchalant and casual as though they're taking some long, enchanted, leisurely Sunday afternoon drive in the country rather than being on the job in an emergency room where sick patients eagerly await their prompt assistance. I just want them to know, for once, how it feels to be at a 22 on a pain scale of 1 to 10, 10 being the worst pain you've ever experienced and have to wait an hour, sometimes as long as two hours, just to be seen. Then wait another hour, an hour and a half, just to receive the pain medication you desperately need—the only thing under the sun that can ease your pain.

By the time they finally give pain relief to you, you've been in pain so long and the pain has elevated to such an intense magnitude the dosage of the medication is inadequate and essentially ineffective. It is so measly measured against the horrifically increased level of the pain; it's more like a joke (being laughed at in the face of the pain). It doesn't help the hurting one iota.

Imagine a busy day on the job—it is noon, and you have a million-and-one things coming at you from every which way; you have an awful headache, but you don't have any Tylenol or Advil on hand to relieve the pain. Now imagine three to four hours later—it's close to quitting time, and your headache has gone from worse to excruciating. By the time you get home, you know that two of anything (short of maybe Valium—a whole 'nother kind of pain reliever) is not going to do the trick. Nine times out of ten, you're going to take three or four Tylenols or Advils to match the level, intensity, and length of time you've been in excruciating pain. Make sense, right? To you, me, and every other reasonably rational, intelligent person but not to most doctors and nurses, however. A lot of them don't get the correlation. They just don't get it, or then again, maybe they get it, but they just don't care about giving proper humane relief!

As I said before, maybe if they experienced even a quarter of the pain I've described, I wouldn't have to wait more than three hours to feel the least bit better, or experience any remote level of relief. I once heard a statement that a dismissed and dissatisfied patient said to a doctor who treated them badly. I quote, "If you ever get ill, I wish you a better doctor than you were to me" (Dorothy Zbornak, *Golden Girls*).

CHAPTER 3

School and Sports

I JUST WANT TO Be Treated the same as other kids.
"Coach, I can play, honest. I really want to do this, please don't say no. Just give me a chance," I pleaded.

"I just don't think that it would be a good idea, Ms. Holder," he replied. "I don't want to be responsible in any way, shape, or form for something happening to you that will jeopardize your health because you're out here fooling around on my court, trying to prove a point."

"That's not fair!" I yelled back. "I'm no different from any of the other girls trying out for the team, so stop treating me like this invalid that is incapable of participating in a game of high school basketball. I'm good, and I want to play for you because you're the best coach I've ever had. I know I can do it, and I know under your coaching, I can get way better than I already am and be a big help to the team. I love this game, and you of all people know that. You can see it in me. You said so yourself."

"Yeah well, that was before I knew you had sickle cell," he hesitantly replied. "And thanks for the compliment, I'm glad you think so highly of my coaching, but flattery is not the key to this gateway," he added with a grimace.

I responded, "No disrespect, but yeah well, my foot! Nothing's changed. I'm still the same person. However unfortunate, sickle cell is what I have, not who I am nor what I am made of or am capable of. It's something I can't help, and it has no bearing on what I am capable of doing, especially once I set my mind to it. I wouldn't be trying so hard or bending over backwards trying to convince you to give me a chance to prove my ability if I didn't think I could do this or if this were not so important to me!"

"Syd, I'm not going to change my mind about this—I mean it—so you're wasting your time," Crutch said.

"Yeah, well, it's my time, so I'll do with it what I want! And what I'm going to do is harass your soul, keep dressing for and coming to pre-tryout practices, and basically stay in your face about this until you change your mind," I bellowed defiantly. "So if you don't want to suffer the aggravation, you might as well give me your consent now, because I will not quit until I get it and you let me on this team! I have what it takes, and you've got what I want, and I'm gonna show you I mean business," I added.

"Saved by the bell!" he exclaimed, as the bell rang loudly and unapologetically above our heads, signaling the beginning of second period classes. "Don't you have a class to get to, Miss 'I wanna be the next Lisa Leslie/Cheryl Swoopes'?" he asked rhetorically, not waiting for a reply. "Now go on, get! You are starting to give me a headache, and it's not even noon yet." He shooed me out of his office with a playful but firm shove to the back.

Goodness! I loved my coach. Everyone did. He was so nice and down to earth, not to mention one of the few black teachers in the entire school. But most of all he was a great coach, proven by one of the best records of the girls' varsity basketball team. He knew when to push you and how to bring the best out of his players and, really, all the kids he came in contact with. He took a genuine interest and really looked out for us. He always had great advice, no matter what the subject matter was. He was like everyone's dad, and that meant a lot, especially to those of us whose fathers were not present in the home.

When he had your back, you knew you'd be OK, especially for the black kids in the school, since we were definitely in the minority when it came to the numbers. But if you screwed up the many chances he gave everyone and, by chance, fell out of his good graces, talk about Siberia, 'cause that's how you felt. With so few of us as compared to the white students and other minority groups, the black kids kind of kept a tight-knit community among the student body and faculty. So if you acted up and got yourself in Siberia, you got everyone's sympathy because Warren Crutchfield was one person you definitely ALWAYS wanted to have in your corner, since he'd put his neck on the line and, if need be, go to bat for you. Everyone in the school knew if Crutch wasn't messing with you, you must've really screwed up multiple times or plain acted a fool, leaving very little hope for you.

He'd taken me under his wing as soon as I came to the school as a freshman, long before my involvement-turned-obsession for basketball. Not to toot my own horn, but I was a good kid, an excellent student academically, and he tended to seek out and pull in students like that. He kept us grounded and always made sure we were doing the best we possibly could in all areas of our academic work.

Screw class, I sighed as I walked down the hall, leaving the gym. How could I be expected to sit in a classroom and focus at a time when my basketball ambitions were in such an uncertain state? All I could and wanted to think about at that time was basketball and the awesome possibility of being given a chance to show Crutch, my friends, the girls on the team, and the rest of the school how good I was on the court. I loved basketball and had for as long as I can remember. I was nine years old when I started watching college hoops like the Georgetown Hoyas, Duke's Blue Devils, Wake Forest's Demon Deacons, and the North Carolina Tar Heels. Georgetown was my favorite at that time, but I knew all the players and their stats regionally and nationally, like Christian Laettner and Grant Hill who played for Duke, Alonzo Mourning, Dikembe Mutombo, and later, Allen Iverson who played for the Hoyas.

He has to say yes. If he doesn't let me be on this team, I will just die, I thought to myself. School would be just another mundane, unexciting task ladled on my plate of life. It would be like having dinner with no dessert and a birthday party with no cake. I had to convince him despite this pain-in-the-ass disease I had hovering over me.

Warren Crutchfield was the varsity basketball coach at my high school. He could be a tough nut to crack, but once you did, he was a softie on the inside. Crutch could be stubborn, but he had yet to find out I can be just as stubborn as the next man until I get what I want. I did end up going to class, but later that afternoon, just as I promised, I was back in the gym, dressed and ready to practice and back in his face. I did all the drills double time, but it was during the freestyle shoot around that I really shone and showed my skills. My three-point game was sweet. I was all over the perimeter with nothing but net. I was even showing up some of the seniors. Ha ha!

Crutch tried to act like he was uninterested and further unimpressed, but I caught him giving me a couple of side glances where his smirk gave way to a half smile he seemed to be trying to choke back. He never let on if he was even remotely impressed with any player. I guess he didn't want our heads to get big in sight of his approval. *Whatever,* I thought to myself. *He can front all he wants.* I knew I was sweet with the ball and would be a valuable addition to the team. I just had to conquer the running of the mile. It was the only thing I was having problems with, but I didn't feel bad because three-fourths of the team were having the same problem. I loved basketball, but I hated running long distances. I'd run the gym with no problem (as long as it wasn't more than ten or twelve laps), but a mile on the football field is endless!

We'd advanced to the second to the last day of tryouts, and Crutch still wasn't paying me any mind. I'd stayed after almost every practice, when everyone else had left, just to hang out with him and see where his head was concerning allowing me on the team, all under the guise of helping him put the equipment away. I'm sure he was on to me and well aware of what I was up to, but so what, I wanted what I wanted—and I was going to get it! There we were on the last day of tryouts, and I started to panic. All that persistence and hard work I put out for him, and it seemed like he wasn't going to give in an inch. I was heated! He'd already cut two girls the day before, but they were some sauce. I mean they sucked, so no one except them were surprised at their demise.

Here we were, down to the wire, and I still had no idea what his call would be. I knew I had done my best, and compared to the rest of the girls, not to toot my own horn, I did better than more than half of them. The other girls acknowledged that as well, so if he had the audacity to say I couldn't be on the team, it would clearly be due to his bias against my illness. I knew I couldn't always perform, but when I could, I did it very well. I was ready to call Johnny Cochran, damn it!

It was hard keeping up with the other kids academically after long absences. Teachers at first would try to patronize me because

I was this "poor, helpless kid." They tried to use my physical limitation to say it was okay if I didn't do as well as the other kids. Also, my peers were constantly questioning why I was always out so much. I felt I had to prove that not only could I do just as well as my peers but I could also do better, even with all my absences, and usually I did.

CHAPTER 4

What Helps the Pain

"TELL ME A story."
        It started with Mom. I would ask her, and when she wasn't around, I would ask whoever was with me, but it had to be someone close to me because an ordinary stranger or someone who didn't know me very well usually wouldn't understand the significance of what storytelling did for my pain or would probably think I was crazy.

When the pain was too much for my mind to cut through, I tried "mind travel." Mind travel or, more appropriately, imagery and a form of meditation is something my mother taught me to help control my pain when I was younger. It is simply the conscious effort of allowing the right brain, which controls creativity and imagination, to take over the left brain, which controls logic, reasoning, and rationalization. It allows your imagination to distract you from the pain.

While going through these "episodes" with me, as my mother so often did, she would instruct me to close my eyes and think of the most beautiful places and things I could possibly imagine. For instance, a vivid sunset blending streaming colors of red, maroon, purple, and orange descending from various shades of blue careening into a sea of halting beauty, almost framing the waves of water as it descends from the heavens. She would tell me to describe to her, in detail, all that my imagination had unleashed. I would do so if the pain was bearable enough to allow me to speak. But if it proved too much to bear to do so, I would remain quiet and still, privately journeying through the specifics of my adventure alone.

During the times when the pain was so excruciating that I could not think straight, let alone bother with imagery, I would ask her to tell me a story while rubbing the paining areas, as I let my mind, body, and soul accompany her on her picturesque narration. I am not saying these techniques quenched my pain entirely, but they certainly took the edge off or, more accurately, my focus off the pain in the interim.

I can't imagine how painful it's been for my mother walking every step of this difficult road with me. Through it all, the hospital stays, the surgeries, the therapies, the recoveries—long, short, and in between, the beginning, middle, and end stages of each and every crisis. She's been to hell and back with me, and through it all, she never gave up on me, faltered, fell short or retreated. I love her most for that. I used to think about the kind of life she could have had if she didn't have the headaches and baggage that came with me and my fateful friend, the Morpher.

I damn near ran her into the poorhouse with all my medical bills. I can't even say *damn near*—hell, I did run her into the poorhouse. I think she gave up or, in some cases, got fired and lost a few good jobs because of all the time off she had to take running behind me when I was younger. Back then, my hospital stays were not every other month like they are now. They were less frequent, about three or four times a year, but when they did take place, I'd sometimes be in the hospital for weeks and, sometimes, months at a time.

I honestly don't know how she did it. The credit bureaus and collection agencies used to ring our phone off the hook, hounding her about all the debts owed the doctors and hospitals she'd accumulated on account of me. She once said to me, "If I must go into the poorhouse, at least I'm going for a more than worthy cause." What was funny was that I didn't feel worthy at all, and for a long time, I hated myself for what I was doing to her life.

Now that I'm older, I've learned to properly channel that hatred. Now I just mostly hate the disease for what it's done to me physically, emotionally, and mentally and, most of all, for what it's done to my family—the pain it caused them to watch me go through it all. She'd always try to hide her worries and fears from me, but I could always see it hidden deep in her eyes, beneath her brave front. Her beautiful smile always came off a little weaker when the slew of medical bills came in the mail or whenever she would take calls from those bill collection people.

Sometimes (after I'd get home from the hospital) late at night, I would hear her crying silently in the next room after she thought I'd gone to sleep. I couldn't have been more than eight or nine, but I knew what was going on. I knew she was crying because of me, and because she loved me so much, she took up my cross. I can't say how many nights I wanted to run into her room, wrap my arms around her, and tell her how sorry I was for being such a burden and for putting her through all this. I wanted to take her face into my little hands, wipe her tears away with my kisses, and tell her it would all be okay. I didn't know how it would be okay or if it ever really would be okay, but I just wanted to hold her and tell her, like she always did with me.

I wanted to thank her for all the long sleepless nights and lonely days she stayed by my side, comforting me, holding my hand, and rubbing different parts of my body when the pain just wouldn't go away. I wanted to thank her for all the times she said she would beg, steal, borrow, and do whatever she had to (and did just that, backed it up with action each and every time) so that I'd always have the best medical care money she didn't have could buy. I wanted to thank her for all the friendships and relationships she sacrificed for me by almost completely giving up her social life because she put me first and foremost on her list of priorities and saw me through. I want to apologize for ruining her life, which I know would've been much easier without me and my baggage.

Since she'd stay with me so often, as soon as I'd arrive, the nurses would set up a cot in my room for her. She was on a first-name basis with the whole staff at Children's Hospital, from the chief of surgery to the cleaning lady. My mother was the kind of lady that once you met her, you'd never forget her. She made you feel like you'd known her your whole life; her spirit was so gentle and magnetic. I'd never seen someone show as much love to a stranger as they would a member of their own family. If you were blessed enough to encounter her, even for a brief moment, in that blink of an eye, somehow she left a piece of her spirit with you, and it was divinely electrifying. Somehow you walked away a better person than you were before. Strangers got to chat it up with her like they were the best of friends. That also rang true from the bottom to the top, from the cleaning lady to the chief of surgery. They never forgot her, and in turn, they never forgot me. I'm almost certain it was because of that they treated me so well. That was partly because if they happened to get on her bad side before they got to her good side, there was hell to pay.

I remember on many occasions, mostly in the emergency rooms, when they would try to dismiss me as a "regular," therefore, no REAL cause for alarm, and we would be kept waiting in chairs for lengthy periods of time, or when the doctor was flippant with her or tried to treat me shabbily. Lord help 'em, cause she would have raised Cain and Jesus Himself if He hadn't risen on his own. Man, when she got to cussing with her accent and all, it was a wrap. I'm pretty sure those doctors and nurses didn't understand half of what she was saying; they just knew by her tone—she meant business and was not to be screwed with!

Back then, and even to this day, it still amazes me to see this petite—no, I mean EXTRA PETITE—firecracker, standing not quite 5 feet, 4 inches tall and weighing a "buck o'five" soaking wet, if that, spring into action when provoked. It's like she becomes a force of nature, a force to be reckoned with, and no one dare try. She's amazing. I remember on numerous occasions when she would get to spittin' fire, I'd be so enthralled by the whole scene for a split moment I'd forget all about the pain and why we were there in the first place.

Through my child's eyes, the level of excitement was comparable to that of watching the characters J. R. Ewing on *Dallas*, Alexis Colby-Carrington on *Dynasty*, and Linda Gray on *Knots Landing* all at the same time, acting a fool and going at their archrival nemesis, back in the day. So you can imagine how I felt. For a little kid, it was like having front-row, ringside tickets to see the Saturday morning WWF (World Wrestling Federation) jump-off with Jimmy "SupaFly" Snocker punishing Hulk "the Hulkster" Hogan with a dropkick to the gut! And the Hulkster countering with a "suplex" (a move where you do a belly flop on top of your opponent and then pin his arm down and his leg up). Needless to say, I used to be a huge WWF wrestling fan back in the days of my youth—never missed a Saturday morning! Only my mom did the punishing with the verbal equivalent of the dropkick to the gut, followed by the suplex, and no one—I mean NO ONE—dared to even attempt to counter her. An angel turned, at the drop of a hat, devil incarnate. She was my hero, and the best part about it was that she was "taking it to the mat" for me.

Now don't get it twisted—those angel-devil-angel exorcisms began to be directed toward me as I got older. At the time, I was beefin' hard with her and would be the first to say we either "didn't mess with each other (tight) like that" or "we didn't ever get along because she always seemed to have an attitude with me!" In hindsight, however, when I'm being truthful with myself about why things really were the way they were, I know her frustration with me surfaced because she didn't believe I was taking care of myself the way I should have been. She constantly reminded me on many occasions of my indifference and belligerent attitude toward my health and how I wasn't doing what it took to stay healthy. At the time I'd deny it or skate around the subject, but now, I will be the first to say, "Yes, I did then, and even now, continue to grow more and more indifferent about my disease and my life, period."

Rightly justified, theoretically or not, from way back then, I began to feel like I was going to keep getting sick, like it or not, no matter what I did or didn't do. Whether I took vitamins or not, whether I ate this or that or didn't eat this or that, whether I went out and played or hung out with friends or not, whether I played sports or I didn't play sports, whether I drank a sea full of water every day or not, it didn't matter! None of those factors seemed to make any difference. Things did not change, nothing did, except maybe not hearing my mom have fits and bitch at me about it so much because over the years, I basically acquired an attitude of indifference. "It is what it is," I used to say to myself. "Might as well do what you want to do for as long as you can do it, before the next episode."

Sometimes, I genuinely did make an effort and tried ALL the things she would tell me and some of what the doctors suggested since they never really advised me on anything along the lines of prevention except maybe trying to convince me to surrender quality for quantity in the form of a cancer drug treatment I vehemently refused. Their advisement came more in terms of "patch 'em up best as ya can" with the proverbial "Band-Aid on a

"THE MORPHER"

broken dam" treatment. Despite all I tried, in the end, none of it made a difference when it came to my crisis.

So yes, you could say I gave up trying to outsmart the monster, because no matter where I hid or what armor I equipped myself with, the game always ended with me trapped in the grips of his jaws. It remained unpredictable, spontaneous, and sporadic in its timing. There were definitely things that angered it and quickened its steps, but once I wised up to those things, I stopped doing them or at least tried my very best consciously not to do them. I knew Mom always just wanted the best for me, and once I was able to see past her anger and frustration, I realized it wasn't directed toward me personally but toward my attitude and the things I would do.

A lot of times my defiance of her anger fueled my recovery. Whenever I did get knocked down, I would hurry, get out of bed, and go out partying once I was home, almost as if to spite her. Almost like saying to her "I can and will get up when I want to, not when you want me to." I had a rebellious yet warped mentality.

Despite all that she saw me go through and all that the doctors predicted of my mortality, she allowed me to do all the things I wanted to. Like when I was about ten years old and I badly wanted a mountain bike and everyone told my mother not to get me the bike because of the Morpher. As always, she preferred to encourage me and not hold me back, so she bought me my lucky-charm bike. Man, was I one happy kid.

When I thought I was mad at her, I was really mad at myself for giving up so easily, especially after seeing how hard she fought for me. But I couldn't bring myself to become hopeful for a change, for the pain to stop, for the intensity or the frequency to decrease. At the time, I thought it was the hope that was my downfall, when it was really my giving up, retreating, accepting, and lying down with the Morpher that was killing me! I prayed to get better not just for myself but for her and, most of all, to defy the gossipers and naysayers.

CHAPTER 5

Contempt and Rage

A NOTHER HORRIFIC INCIDENT occurred more recently, at what I thought, prior to my experience, was a good hospital. Obviously for legal reasons, I'm not going to name names, so we'll call it XYZ General.

Early Saturday morning, around 2:00 a.m., I was driving home from a friend's house after a mild evening of socializing, eating, and seeing some old friends at a graduation after-party celebration, when suddenly, out of nowhere, I was gripped with the familiar pain of my frequent friend, the Morpher (sickle cell crisis).

It was a twenty-minute drive from Columbia, Maryland, to Gaithersburg, so I immediately downed some over-the-counter pain medication I usually carry around in my purse for just such an emergency. I tried not to think about the pain as it intensified and traveled swiftly yet methodically through my body as though plotting a revolt. Within less than ten minutes, my rigid body was completely gripped by pain with a severity I had not experienced in quite some time.

My chest felt like someone had kicked me dead center with the sole of a steel-toed army boot and was standing on the bull's-eye of their fallen target. It became increasingly difficult for me to breathe with every inhale-exhale exchange. I began gasping out of a necessity to get enough air in my lungs. I, also, tried not to move too much, which would further aggravate the already ferocious pain that seemed to be eating away at every cell, bone, and muscle in my body. With limited control over my limbs, the pain having decreased my mobility and ability to respond considerably, I slowed the car to a mere 25 miles/hr. I'm sure if there had been any other cars on Highway 270 with me I would have received a fair amount of obscene gestures most likely coupled with a roll of profane language harsh enough to make a sailor blush. Thankfully, with this whole scenario taking place during the wee hours of the morning, there was no one else on the highway, save for your random night riders here and there.

The pain had traveled to both my arms, feeling as though I'd lost a violent game of tug-of-war and the victor had broken both of my humeri in half and again at the elbows. I could barely hold the wheel in my hands as it became increasingly difficult to hold my arms up. To make matters worse, my car, a 5-speed compact, needed to be nursed on the road by incessant up-and-down shifting of the clutch and gear stick. I couldn't have been in a worse position physically. Any movement at the onset of these attacks ultimately determines the intensity and severity of the pain, as well as where and how fast it travels throughout my body. Thus, driving a 5-speed car, with all that's required of one's motor skills, is not the kind of moving you want to be engaged in when your whole body's literally shutting down on you, as was the case for me. My legs felt like I was bouncing a small child up and down on them, playing teeter-totter, only, this "child" weighed upwards of 200 lbs. It became increasingly harder to move my feet the few inches to the right or to the left of their resting position as required to maneuver the clutch-stick reflex and juggle the accelerator and brakes. At one point, I just gave up completely and decided to coast down the I-270 highway without doing a thing for as long as the temperament of the road would allow.

By this time, the eight or nine pills I had washed down with half a bottle of warm Gatorade retrieved from the backseat fifteen minutes earlier seemed to have the effect equivalent to that of throwing back a handful of Smarties sugar candy that children had used back in the day when playing doctor. It had done nothing at all except leave a lingering wave of nausea in the pit of my stomach, as the acids and juices surrounding them struggled to dissolve and provide the familiar analgesic. Over-the-counter drugs . . . what did I expect? It was obvious this demonic pain, a remnant of—but surpassing that of—Linda Blair's tumultuous vomit-spewing head spin scene in *The Exorcist* was not going to, would not submit to, anything short of the real McCoy. Ooh yeah . . . They were definitely going to have to pull out the big guns once I arrived in the ER. *That is, if I ever make it*, I thought. It seemed the closer

I got to Gaithersburg, the further away it became. And to think, at the initial onset of the pain storm, I had actually toyed with the idea of dragging my limp, pain-riddled body home, up three flights of stairs, into my condo and into my bed. Yeah right! Who was I kidding! I wouldn't have made it up the first step, let alone three flights!

I tried to relax (my body), but the pain was too much for my mind to cut through. By now it was at the forefront of my whole being, holding every cell in my body hostage for a ransom to be paid by the only thing that, from this point on, would bring relief—heavy NARCOTIC pain medication. Narcotics like Morphine, Demoral, Dilaudid—hell, at that moment, I'd have settled for a horse tranquilizer. Given the seated position I was in, trying to relax was no easy feat. My long legs seemed entangled among the pedals that obstructed their ability to extend fully, causing them to pretzel uncomfortably as the pain rifled up, down, around, and through my bones. I decided to try mind travel. *At this point, what could it hurt?* I thought to myself.

I wish my mother had been with me during this particular visit to the ER, because it proved to be one of the worst hospital experiences I've ever encountered to date.

Save for the grace of God, I don't quite know how I arrived at the hospital in one piece (if you could call it that), but when I finally did, I was a complete mess. I was in so much pain I couldn't think straight. It took me a good ten minutes to open the car door, erect my body, swing my legs around and out of the car, and finally, to pull myself upright while holding on to the car door for dear life. Hunched over, dragging my uncooperative legs along, inch by inch, I finally made it through the sliding glass doors of the emergency room to the ER admit desk, which stood about forty feet away from the entrance, where I ultimately collapsed, just as the young red-haired gentleman behind the desk asked me, "Are you okay? Do you need help? Did someone come with you? What is the matter?" and if I'd been to that hospital before— respectively. Barely able to keep up with the string of interrogation, I opted to answer the most important question (to me, anyway), "Yes, I have been here before, and I'm having a sickle cell crisis— please help me," I replied weakly. By this time, it was about two

"THE MORPHER"

thirty, quarter to three in the morning, so the ER waiting area was virtually deserted—only in the 'burbs, which is an accurate description of where we were geographically. He ran around to the other side of his post, grabbing a wheelchair in the process, which he whirled around just in time to scoop me up before my backside hit the cold linoleum floor. He looked me over with empathy, as though trying to imagine the degree of pain behind the agonizing and disconcerted expression pasted on my twisted and distorted face. "What's your social, sweetheart?" he queried in a soothingly gentle tone. I barely managed to audibly relay the numbers to my social security as he requested. Somehow he was able to dissect and process the jumbled utterance I spewed past my partly clenched teeth because with the snap of a finger, he produced a hospital identification armband, which I assumed contained the necessary vital statistics. Surprisingly, he never even asked me what my name was. Though I found that rather unusual, I was in no position to inquire about, let alone contest, his actions. I would later learn, in retrospect, it should not have been surprising that he did not process the correct social security number, therefore rendering me a fraudulent patient, of which I would soon stand accused.

After placing the band around my arm, he hurriedly transported me to the triage area to be physically assessed and where they would ultimately determine if I legitimately required further emergency care. When I was deposited in the cold, tiny, and uninviting room, which housed a scale, blood pressure, and temperature machine among other technical-looking contraptions, I was reluctantly received by a sullen, middle-aged, very abrasive-looking woman I presumed to be the triage nurse. She looked much older than she probably was. I pegged her to be in her early- to midfifties, although the hardness in her face, where stress and the weight of life had obviously taken its toll, appeared at least sixty plus—well into retirement range. Her salt-and-pepper-colored coif seemed to grip her scalp in a mound of unending tight curls. Undoubtedly, whoever the culprit was that had roller-set her hair had left her under the hair dryer a tad too long, because her hairdo tagged her a cross between the third Stooge, Curly, and Richard Simmons. They had set her up big-time. I guess if I had to walk around with my hair looking like Thelma Harper from the TV show *Mama's Family*, I'd be pissed at the world myself, to say the least.

As I sat there momentarily lost in thought, trying to wish away the whole agonizing experience, the force with which she grabbed my arm abruptly and painfully brought me back to the harsh reality of where I was and why I was there. I glared at her with disapproving eyes as she attempted to secure a blood pressure cuff around my arm, hoping to make eye contact with her and confirm that she was, in fact, hurting me, since she was ignoring the moaning and wincing that pierced the air in the otherwise silent room, indicative of the excruciating pain I was in. Her chestnut-colored eyes seemed to bear no life, as though there was no one home, with no remnants of her existence except the empty shell that sat before my very eyes, simply going through the motions.

"Where's your pain, miss?" she finally crooned in a dry, uninterested tone.

"ALL OVER, you friggin' idiot, are you blind or just stupid?" I wanted to scream but managed to control my frustration for her contemptuous attitude, rough nature, and snail's pace before it spewed from my lips like molten lava.

"My pain is all over," I tearfully retorted. That was about as close to calm as I could muster under the circumstances. "It's in both arms, both legs, and most intense in my chest, in the area of my sternum and in my lower back, slightly below my kidneys, only it's more centered. On a scale of 1 to 10, it's about a 20 in severity."

Maybe she would take me seriously now that I'd broken it down to her in a manner that proved not only was I no amateur at this but also that I was extremely intelligent and equally articulate. Not one to be patronized or taken lightly, because I knew more about what was going on with me than she would ever hope to learn in a lifetime. Her skepticism was apparent, and she seemed decisively biased, undoubtedly on the mere basis of my appearance and attire.

I was coming from a party, and therefore, I had on a dressy-casual black strappy camisole-like top, a pair of loose-fitting, black capri pants, and high-heeled sandals. My hair was all done up, and although I had been crying, my makeup was essentially still intact. So yes, I probably did look like I was en route to a club, not sick and in the intense pain I professed to be in; however, it still should have had no bearing on the quality of care she was being paid to administer. I don't care if I came in a skintight black leather hooker outfit with chains and a whip hanging from my belt; it shouldn't have made a difference either way. It wasn't the first time someone doubted I was sick, let alone had a debilitating illness, thereby wanting to deny me medical attention, and I'm sure it would not be the last.

While she dawdled through a barrage of unending questions such as what brought the attack on and how long it had been since my last crisis (rather unenthusiastically, as though she was sitting on her couch on a rainy Sunday afternoon, skimming idly through the TV guide because she had nothing better to do), the excruciating pain and her obvious lack of interest, began to get the better of me. But again, out of all those questions, she, as well, never asked me my name. As she was filling out what looked to be some sort of form—I'm guessing patient history—she reached out and looked at my armband and continued writing.

As she poked and prodded, taking my temperature, making me stand on the cold scale propped against the far wall, even after I told her I couldn't because it was too painful to move, I began to get agitated. My body began internally convulsing uncontrollably as the pain intensified from all the moving she was making me do. It was clearly obvious by her unsympathetic demeanor she had never even remotely treated or dealt with anyone with sickle cell disease or she would have known that her unwarranted actions served only to increase my discomfort, thereby making me less cooperative and her job ultimately more difficult. Either that or she just didn't care because I was just another obstruction interfering with her desire to sit on her ass and do nothing until her shift was over and it was time to punch out.

All I wanted for her to do was wheel me back to the part of the emergency room where I could receive some *real* assistance, preferably in the form of gentle patient care, intravenous fluids to counter the cell sickling process, and pain relief. Instead, she wheeled me back into the uninviting, deserted hallway where I was made to wait another forty-five minutes before anyone showed any interest in me again.

SYDATU HOLDER

Boy, if this particular trip didn't drive home anything else, it sure taught me and drove home the point that I should NEVER, EVER, EVER, EVER come to a place like that alone and on my own—which I already knew, but there I was, trying to brave it out by myself as usual. If I had been brought in by ambulance, I wouldn't even have had to deal with this unpleasant troll, but again, like many times before, I wanted minimal drama, attention, and hassle. It seemed either way, I couldn't win!

At last, Cruella the Bad Witch wheeled me back to the real emergency room area, where they actually treated people instead of wasting their time. I was then received by a young lady that looked to be in her late twenties, early thirties, with sandy-brown hair that was swept up in an impromptu bun, resting comfortably just below the crown of her head. She had strikingly beautiful blue eyes, I think the kindest I'd ever seen. Obviously she represented the warmer, friendlier version of XYZ's hospital staff. Not like the mutt I'd just been exposed to, with an attitude that clearly indicated she was long overdue for a colonic. Her name was Julie, and she had the most captivating smile. I remember because she actually tried to be comforting, her smile exuding true sincerity and showing genuine concern and understanding.

As she wheeled me from the triage room, she said, "Don't worry, sweetheart, we're gonna take good care of you. As soon as I get you situated in a bed, I'll get the doctor to give you something for the pain." She had a sweet smile and a laid-back Southern drawl to match that flowed as easy as a lazy Weeping Willow. For just a moment, it made me nostalgically think of my folks in the A-T-L, HotLanta.

Those words were like music to my ears. I was tempted to grab her, give her a big hug and kiss, and proposition my firstborn out of sheer gratitude. But in lieu of any future embryos, I weakly flashed her the best smile I could muster. Well, at least the best I had to offer at the time.

After this brief moment of absolution, I dropped my head slightly, taking notice of the green-and-white checkered pattern of the polished-and-buffed-to-a-high-shine tile floor, as the wheelchair glided through the chill of the air-conditioned hallway. In bringing my head back up, I noticed that not only did the ride seem longer than I recalled it being in the past but we were also going to an entirely different area of the hospital. Unfamiliar territory that obviously attempted to soothe and ease the impending anxiety of its visitors with its cheerful decor of pink, brown, and green giraffes on the wall and coordinating animal curtains. All of which I certainly did not mind because it was a very welcomed pleasantry from the norm, but something just seemed off in a major way. I hadn't seen hospital decor like this since I was younger and a rightful occupant of the pediatric unit. *The pediatric unit!* I thought to myself with alarm. Were they full or overcrowded in the general ER ward, or was I a delusional victim of the twilight zone?

I felt like any minute I would see the big black-and-white swirling, hypnotic ring they used to show at the introduction of the television show *The Twilight Zone.* You know, the image they showed right before the clip of this Caucasian woman holding her hands to her face and letting out a thrilling shriek—okay, so I'm overdramatizing, so sue me. I started to relay an objection to my whereabouts, but by that point, I just wanted to stretch my pain-invaded body out on the too-small cot version of a bed, which at that point would feel like a king-size pillow-top at the Waldorf Astoria, and cooperate long enough to get some pain-relieving treatment. I was in too much agony to even think of rocking the boat, so I kept my mouth shut and decided to go along for the ride until someone could fill me in on what was really going on.

Once we arrived in the curtained-off area I assumed would be my temporary resting area for the time being, Julie helped me out of the wheelchair and onto the tiny stationary gurney in the middle of the room and gave me a hospital gown to change into. I was considerably taller and bigger than her tiny frame so, as not to overpower her, I tried to pull the bulk of my weight onto the bed myself, unsuccessfully ending up with half my body hanging awkwardly off the edge.

As she hurried out of the room, she turned swiftly and said, "You go ahead and change into that gown, and I'll be back in a minute to ask you a few questions before I get the doctor to give you something for the pain."

I quietly nodded in agreement as I tried to straighten my body on the gurney enough to allow me to sit up, take my top off, and put the gown on before she returned. My goodness, it seemed every inch I moved invited excruciating ripples of pain that washed over my body like a tidal wave. *I better hurry,* I thought to myself as the thimble-sized bit of energy I had left quickly depleted. My breathing continued to become increasingly labored until I was again gasping for air. At that point, I just said to myself, *The hell with changing, I'll do it when I get something for the pain and get more comfortable,* and commenced to lie back down, as still as possible, and wait for Julie to return.

She couldn't have been gone too long, but it seemed like forever. It was now almost four fifty in the morning. Thereby, I'd been in incessant pain for almost three hours with no relief since I'd arrived at the hospital shortly after 2:00 a.m. Those pills I took on my way to the hospital certainly had not made any difference whatsoever to the pain I was feeling.

Julie returned within a few minutes of her initial departure, which was remarkable, considering that in ER time, a few minutes usually ends up being closer to an hour. She was turning out to be one of the best emergency room nurses I'd encountered in a long time, and with my hospital track record, I'd encountered more nurses and doctors per year than most people do in two lifetimes—and that's during a good year.

"The doctor will be in shortly," she said. "But first, I just need to ask you a few questions." At that point, what could I really say? "No! No more damn questions. Doctor, drugs—NOW!" *If only,* I thought. *Just make it quick, toots,* I thought. *My nine lives are expiring rapidly, and I'm running out of what little steam, patience, and cooperative spirit I had to begin with.* "Okay," I grimaced instead.

"So you've been here before, huh? When was your last visit?" she questioned.

Visit! I thought. It was a legitimate question, but this chick made it sound like a day trip to the damn zoo! Was she serious? As sweet as she'd been to me, in my state of mind and present condition, I wanted to reach out and shake the @#$% out of her, hopefully rattling her common-sense marbles back into place, and hollering, "Does this look like a leisurely experience here? Wake up!" I know I was just being testy and impatient, but I'm not one for many words, stupidity, or time wasting when I'm in this state. But I mean really, who would be? No more stupid connotations! I couldn't take it.

I just smirked, "A couple of years ago maybe—I think it was back in 2002. I can't recall exactly, but I'd just moved back to the area," I said, with a twinge of edge in my voice. I know she was only doing her job and trying to help, but like everyone else, she was beginning to work on my nerves. It seemed like I'd answered these same stupid question a zillion times. I thought this was the whole purpose of hospital records. Hello!

"So you've had this problem since . . ." Her voice trailed, suggesting she wanted me to finish her sentence.

I bit. "All of my life," I obliged.

"And you're seventeen now, right?" she said rhetorically.

"Seventeen!" Was she on crack! Where the hell did she come up with that crap! I didn't know whether to be flattered at the compliment of looking that youthful or to be further annoyed by the obvious incompetence, further proving this hospital really did suck.

"Uh . . . no, far from—" I stammered, my voice displaying my obvious expression of bewilderment, quickly followed by exasperation and annoyance.

"Why would you think I was seventeen, do I look that young?" I asked.

"As a matter of fact, you do, but that's what it says here on your chart." As though it were contagious, the same puzzled expression and confusion washed over her face.

"That's impossible," I retorted. "There's no way—I'm not seventeen, and I haven't been for a good long time."

"You are Jessica Benjamin, aren't you?" she hesitantly questioned.

"Jessica who . . . who's Jessica? I'm not Jessica. My name is Syd Holder," I said matter-of-factly.

"Well, it says here, you're Jessica, age seventeen, 12890 Sheldon Place, Gaithersburg, Maryland. So you're saying you're not Jessica Benjamin," she asked again.

This was getting out of control! "Trick, are you hooked on phonics?" I wanted to scream. *Isn't that what I just said?*

"No, my name is Syd Holder. My driver's license and social security card are in my purse. Please get it out so you can see for yourself if you don't believe me," I firmly stated. My confusion was now quickly turning into exasperation.

"Is that what you told triage, because it's obvious someone thinks you are Jessica Benjamin and not Syd Holder," she exclaimed as she reached into my wallet, retrieved my driver's license and social security cards, and confirmed their validity. "I wonder what's going on—how could this happen?" she asked out loud.

"I don't know. I certainly never told anyone that I was Jessica whoever or anything remotely like that. I didn't tell them anything!" I explained. "The guy at the admissions desk just asked if I had been here before, I told him yes I had. Then he asked for my social security number as he helped me into this wheelchair"—I pointed to the chair, still resting just in front of the bed. "I gave him my social, he didn't say anything else to me, or ask me any more questions—not my name, nothing. Two seconds later, he came around to my chair, put this band around my wrist, and wheeled me straight back to the triage nurse. The only other statement he made was that he hoped I felt better. He didn't say anything else, he didn't ask anything else, and furthermore, I was in so much pain, I didn't think to question or check the band because I figured, he must have been able to pull up all the information he needed from my social security number as had been done many times before," I exclaimed.

"That's why it was not strange to me that he didn't even ask me my name, only my social security number, which is not unusual. It's been done like that here, in this very hospital, at least a dozen times in the past, because most of the time people can't pronounce my name to begin with," I explained further. "But nothing like this identity mix-up or whatever has ever happened to me before."

"Okay, sit tight," she said. "Let me find out what's going on, and I'll be back in a minute."

"But . . . but what about the pain? It's so bad, and it's getting worse," I cried. By this time, fresh tears had begun to fall, not just the whine that sometimes substitutes when you've cried so much 'til you can't cry anymore, when you're literally all cried out—out of pain but mostly out of pure frustration.

"I'm sorry, hon," she said, "I can't get any orders written for you until we get this straightened out. But I promise I'll try not to be too long. I'll be as quick as I possibly can."

I thought I was going to die if I had to wait a second longer for some pain medication. The pain was so out of control. Was her promise supposed to ease the excruciating pain that was coursing through my body? Was it supposed to bring me comfort or sustain me? Well, damn it, it didn't, so don't "hon" me like that's supposed to sweeten the pot, I wanted to yell after her! I know she was just doing her job, but I was becoming increasingly unnerved and frustrated with all the bureaucracy and BS, and could you blame me?

When she returned the third time, she didn't look happy at all. She quickly stated, "Okay, hon, we're gonna have to move you out of the peds ward and into the general ER," as she proceeded to put the bedrails up and release the wheel brakes on the gurney. By then, every part of my body was screaming from the pain; even my hair hurt. I started to interject and remind her that I was in excruciating pain that had become absolutely unbearable, but I could tell by the empathetic look she stared at me with that she already knew or, at the very least, had an idea of how bad I felt. She pushed the room-dividing curtain back and pulled the long cot into the sterile corridor. As she wheeled the bed down the hall, I mentally waved good-bye to the animated giraffes that danced on the walls and curtains—I bid farewell to tranquility and buried myself further under the thin white sheet as the cold, brisk air wrapped around me as the rolling cot picked up speed.

A minute later, we were back in the general population. Although my eyes were shut tight, I could tell by the pungent, overpowering, and intrusive Pine-Sol ammonia-like scent of sterility that vastly differed from the less offensive, more pleasant scent of the pediatric unit we'd left behind. Hopefully, we had arrive at what I hoped would be my final destination, at least for a while, until I felt a little better. The tiny curtained-off cubicle was about the same size as the one I just vacated but far less appealing.

The drabness of the room was depressing. The floor tiles were not the clean white they were in the ped unit. The floors in this part of the ER were a dingy mid-green-leaf color of tile that was as unflattering as a fat lady in a tube top. Complementing the ugly floors were pale-green curtains that stretched around the three corners of the room in a U-shaped fashion. As my eyes spanned the parameter of the small space, I was repulsed by one of the dingy curtain panels, where you could plainly see a long trailed line of what must have been blood splatter that'd long since dried. Did they really expect people to feel better or recover in this poorly masked infestation of filth? Ugh!

Julie must have caught on to the sour look plastered on my face, accompanied by my wrinkled nose, because she said, as if on cue, "It's not so bad, and hopefully you'll be out of here soon. In the meantime, why don't you try to relax and get some rest while I try to get some orders from the doctor for you."

"The pain is too much, my chest is hurting. I can't—I . . . I feel like I can't breathe. Julie, ple-please help me," I cried out as I reached for her.

I needed pain medicine—fast—but I didn't want her to leave me. Admittedly, my usual tough-as-nails facade had melted away with the pain, leaving me feeling vulnerable, like a scared little kid that was all alone, which in a sense, I was.

Trying to be consoling, Julie said, "I know, hon, I know. Just hang in there a little while longer for me, okay?" she said as she rubbed my shoulder.

How could I be upset with her? After all, she was being so nice about everything. I certainly wasn't thrilled about the mix-up, but the gentle way she handled it made going through the whole ordeal a little easier than if she'd been a bitch about it—I'd have had to cut her then! Little did I know this was a cakewalk compared to what lay ahead.

As nice as Julie had been to me, I felt like I was about to lose it, "kirk out," and start screaming like crazy people in mental institutions are notorious for. You know, freakish, delusional cries directed at no one in particular. Pleas like "Help me, somebody help me, please" at the top of my lungs. I must have subconsciously scared Julie off with all the silent screaming and crying I was doing because she never came back.

Instead, I was accosted by the Terminator, a bleached blond, leathery-skinned, thin-lipped heifer I like to refer to as Freda Krueger—you know, next of kin to Freddy—who returned in her place. Her yellowish platinum hair, which hung lifelessly around her shoulders, stopped midway down her back. While her rough, prematurely wrinkled, and tawny-colored complexion made it sadly evident she'd spent a few too many hours on the tanning bed. All this seemed to contribute to her tight-lipped, snubbed-nose, unwelcoming demeanor.

She walked in abruptly and declared, "Okay, Jessica, Cy-dada, or whatever you're going by today, you're going to have to leave now!"

Was this witch for real? I thought. Either this really was turning into my *Nightmare on Elm Street* or this fool must've tripped and bumped her head, and if she hadn't, I was ready to help her real quick!

"Wh-haat?" I stuttered, the sound of my voice muffled by the two blankets that were draped over my weak body. "What did you say?" I repeated, more audibly this time.

"I said get up, missy. It's time for you to go right now. You don't have to go home, but you're certainly not staying here," she said nastily.

"What do you mean I have to go? I'm sick! I'm having a sickle cell crisis and I need help," I retorted, trying to stay calm so as not to aggravate the pain more than it already was.

With her hands planted firmly on her hips, she hissed, "Well, I'm sorry, we don't treat liars or anyone under fraudulent circumstances, so you're gonna have to leave."

I was in shock! Stunned by the words I heard coming from this she-devil who didn't know me from Adam but, from the time she laid eyes on me and from the start of the conversation, seemed to have it in for me. I felt like someone had walked up to me and slapped me in the face without warning. My eyes stung with fresh tears as the hurtfulness of her words settled in.

"Fraudulent circumstances." What on earth was she talking about? Was she allowed to do this, treat people that desperately needed help and a little compassion, like they were dirt or trash off the street? I thought to myself.

"What do you mean 'fraudulent circumstances,' what are you talking about?" I said. My bewilderment didn't seem to faze her at all.

"I'm referring to you lying about your identity. We do not deal with anyone under such conditions, therefore, we are not going to render any treatment to you. Now you'll have to leave—we need the bed," she said sternly, as she neared my purse and shoes that were sitting on the counter in the back of the small room. For a minute I thought she was going to throw them at me, as she quickly gathered them up and placed them at the foot of the gurney.

"Are you serious? I can't leave. Where am I supposed to go? I can't even walk. I'm sick and I'm in too much pain to even move—I need help. Please help me,' I pleaded in desperation.

"I don't know what to tell you, and it's not my problem. Whoever brought you here or however you got here is the same way you're going to have to leave and go someplace else. Now go ahead and get dressed," she answered.

"Why are you doing this? I didn't lie to anyone about anything, I swear to you."

The pain was on a rampage like a five-alarm fire. It invaded my entire body with a rekindled vengeance. I was already distressed, and the added stress of her unfounded and threatening accusations was the last thing I needed. This was not the way things were supposed to go. I couldn't believe any of this was really happening.

They're not supposed to treat sick people like this! It felt like I was having a bad dream I couldn't wake up from. There's nothing worse than being accused of something you didn't do. And in this case, the circumstances magnified the injustice to the nth degree. This was not the time to have to deal with this crap. I was in no condition to squabble with anyone, let alone this viper of a wench.

As she proceeded to exit the room, I reached out my arm and said, "Wait! Please, just wait a minute—if you don't believe me, just ask the guy at the front admissions desk by the triage entrance. He was the only one I talked to. He was the one that took all of my information, put it into the computer, and gave me this band before wheeling me back into the triage room. He can corroborate my story and tell you exactly what happened, since you don't believe me."

"What guy—what's his name?" she said impatiently.

"I don't know his name, but he's white, and I think he had reddish-brown hair—from what I could tell. He's medium build, with freckles and glasses. I don't recall what he had on exactly, but he must work in ER admissions because he was sitting behind the desk when I first arrived. Please just talk to him and ask him yourself, you'll see."

"There is no guy at the admissions desk," she interjected.

"But you haven't even bothered to go out and check, so how can you say that—how do you know?"

"I don't have to go and check. I know there is no guy at the desk now," she said impatiently. "And frankly, I don't have time for your shenanigans. There are people that are really sick here that need my attention!" she continued.

"Well, where's Julie? I want to talk to Julie—she'll help me," I snapped.

"Julie can't help you now. Besides, she's already left," she sneered. It almost seemed as though she was enjoying my predicament! Now I really wanted to slap her. I couldn't believe it. I lay quiet for a moment, and then it hit me. *Dammit, the shifts must have changed*, I thought to myself. That's why Julie was gone and I was left to deal with this piece of work, and if Julie was gone, that meant the guy at the front admissions desk who registered me (or more like screwed me up the creek without a paddle) and gave me the incorrect band must be gone too!

I looked at my watch, and things began to make sense. It was six forty in the morning. Just about every hospital—at least all the ones I frequented anyway—change or rotate their shifts at 7:00 a.m., 3:00 p.m., and again at 11:00 p.m. Most nurses usually started wrapping up their duties and began doing their paperwork a half hour or so before their shift was scheduled to end or begin. Around the same time, the incoming shift of nurses would be there to get their assignments and, usually in the case of the emergency room, acquaint themselves with the remaining active charts/patients that had not been discharged or admitted for further care and transfer upstairs.

So Nurse Ratchet was right. The guy that was posted at the emergency room front desk when I arrived couldn't vouch for me nor confirm my story. He wasn't there. Since there was still at least twenty minutes left before the shift officially changed, she could have tried to find the guy from the emergency desk if she really wanted to. She just wanted to be a witch about the whole thing.

I was screwed, or so she thought. I knew in my heart that I had done nothing wrong; therefore, I was rightfully entitled to proper medical attention, and though she wasn't willing to give it to me, I wasn't giving up—I couldn't.

I answer to and rely on a higher power who promised to never leave me nor forsake me, so I called on Him in silent prayer. During my moment of silent meditation, Nurse Ratchet had departed from the room without a word.

I lay quietly, trying to regain some semblance of composure and regroup from the unnecessary aggravation. As I focused my thoughts on things peaceful and tranquil, in an attempt to divert my attention away from the excruciating pain I was still in and had been in for the last four, going on five, hours, a feeling of relief washed over me, and somehow I knew everything would turn out for my good.

Less than fifteen minutes later, a doctor walked in, spieled the usual medical rhetoric involving the when, where, and why of the pain crisis I was having, then assured me that I would be getting something for the pain real soon. Words I'd been longing to hear for the past four hours. Just like that! Needless to say, I never saw what's-her-face again!

Before he could make his departure though, I interjected, in an attempt to address the abrasive treatment I'd been subjected to at the hand of the bleached-blond, leather-skinned, tight-lipped wench who had the audacity to call herself a nurse. I told him that I was not, by any means, there under fraudulent circumstances and that I had not then, nor ever before, lied about who I was. I went on to announce to him that I had rights, that I was not ignorant and knew those rights, and therefore, could not and should not be denied proper medical care nor treated in the manner that I had been treated.

Before I could continue my declaration of life, liberty, freedom, and the pursuit of happiness, he abruptly cut me off—stopped me dead in my tracks—and said dryly, without so much of a hint of empathy or sincerity, "The matter will be looked into." And, as if holding two completely different conversations with two entirely different people, addressing two totally unrelated issues, he abruptly interjected, "We're going to need to start an IV and get a urine sample." Looked into by whom and when will this so-called investigation commence? is what I wanted to know!

How do you like that! If pain relief hadn't been part of that offer, I'd have had to go into my "You'll be hearing from my attorney" speech and borderline threat. But relief was pending, so I decided to revisit the issue at a later, more opportune (to my well-being) time.

I can't even say I remember the guy's name—the doctor, that is. At such a critical time when I should have been taking names, titles, and other pertinent statistics to file a formal complaint or do something in terms of gaining some retribution, I dropped the ball or, rather, let it go for the time being anyway. Like I said before, I chose to and decided to trust in my Guy upstairs, who outranked all of their guys—and everyone else, for that matter—down here.

I was hurt. I felt betrayed and abused, but most of all, I was angry. I was angry that people truly in need of medical attention could be treated so inhumanely as though they were second-class citizens, undeserving of the same level of respect, unworthy of the same quality of care as anyone else of, say, a higher stature, income bracket, social standing, or class.

I don't know what the premise of the treatment I received during that particular visit to the hospital fell under. I have turned it over in my mind at least a million times. If I were a white lady, if I had better health insurance—or any health insurance for that matter—or if I were this or that, would I have been treated differently? Even though it's well into the twenty-first century, where racism is supposed to be a thing of the past and sexism remedied, upon closer examination of the society in which we all

SYDATU HOLDER

reside, in truth, these problems and other prejudices still exist, though not as overtly apparent as our past history illustrated.

People just don't care anymore. It's all about the bottom line, PROFIT! Got health insurance, you can expect somewhat decent care. No insurance, yup. You can pretty much count on crappy care all around the board, including the time of day doctors will give you, their level of interest and care, to how you get treated when admitted in the hospitals.

The humiliation and degradation that I have experienced in each and every hospitalization episode has never changed throughout all my instances of bouts with this disease. It is one thing that has always been and, more than likely, will never change. I've been made to feel like I'm not a person with feelings, emotions, intelligence, and integrity who deserves the respect of medical personnel. Or, as my mother would say, I am manhandled at my most vulnerable moments.

Some doctors and nurses hurt you and are physically, emotionally, and mentally abusive to you. They bruise your ego instead of trying to uplift you. While you're physically incapacitated, they crush you and mash you down further into the ground.

And if you're like me, you take the pain, swallow it, push it down, and shove the pain so deep down until you're a walking time bomb, distrustful and cynical toward anyone wearing a white coat, scrubs, and a stethoscope until finally you just kick the hell out of the injustice, mistreatment, and manhandling.

No one ever really apologized for the fraud accusations.

The patient advocate lady came by later to placate me, expressing her shock and fake (that's how I interpreted it anyway) concern about the situation with promises of further action and investigation. None of which ever happened. Nothing was followed up on or done about the mistreatment. My thoughts and desire was to seek legal recourse.

I was dealing with my pain and had no one to stand up for me or on my behalf, like following up and making sure someone was held accountable as Mommy would have done had she been around.

I tried reaching out to Tante for help, understanding, and ACTION since she's a medical doctor herself. But Tante's attempted help came out in a weak and passive sort of way. She basically told me, not in so many words, to forget about it—it happens. I was so very angry and HURT! In this particular instance and, overall, on a broader scale, people are mistreated, used, abused, and disrespected in the health-care system very often these days.

I vowed never to set foot in XYZ hospital again.

A few days after being admitted, when I finally came to and was reflecting on the situation in the ER, which still very much disturbed me, I couldn't help but wonder if and how things would have unfolded if I were a young white patient suffering from symptoms similar to mine and in just as much pain. I don't like to think about events or things in my life in terms of race. However, I would be naive to think that even in this day and age, with all the so-called social progress this country has supposedly made, that race is no longer ever a factor in such circumstances and issue.

I felt ashamed of my disease, of having the kind of disease that was unknown for the longest time and, in many instances, is still mostly unknown.

CHAPTER 6

Divine Intervention

I WAS BROUGHT UP in the church, and from an early age, I have always been very conscientious of the presence of God in my life. My mother is of the Episcopalian denomination, and my father—well, let's just say he was not a church regular, but I believe he was a Presbyterian. My grandmother, a Lord-loving and God-fearing woman with the firm belief that God is always in control, definitely enriched my spiritual development and had a great impact on my spirituality very early on. When most Christian children were just learning to recite their "Now I lay me down to sleep" bedtime homage to God, not necessarily knowing exactly the whys and whats of what they were saying, only that maybe their parents told them that is what good little boys and girls did if they wanted to get in to heaven, I was far beyond that.

Having an illness such as mine, I started crying out to God from as young as I can remember, and I still cry out to Him to this very day, except in a much louder wail. I respect those of different faiths, with different beliefs and values from mine. However, I cannot conceive how anyone with any kind of problem or who has experienced any kind of pain in their lifetime can possibly not know God and believe in Him. I even respect atheists but I just flat-out don't understand them. In my personal case, because of God, I am alive.

I knew Jesus lived and was as real as the air I breathed when, at any one moment, I would be gravely ill, lying in a hospital bed with fevers in the 100s and up and infections up the wazoo. I'm talking urinary tract infection, kidney infection, pneumonia, and sometimes all at the same time. I mean I would be sick as a dog, sometimes so much so my skin would have a yellow or green discoloration to it. I glowed, for crying out loud! I'd have tubes coming out of every end of me from three or four IVs; I'd lose five to ten pounds at a time. Are you getting the picture?

Then when I finally would be released after being in the hospital, sometimes for a period of no less than *several* weeks to months (NOT JUST ONE MONTH, BUT MONTHS— plural), I'd go home, and after about the second or third day, I'd be back to almost better than new. I mean, people used to think I was lying about the gravity and seriousness of my illness. They could not believe that I, the person they had just visited in the hospital a few days prior, looked so good, sometimes even better than I did before I went in the hospital so gravely ill, after only a couple of days home. I mean at the rate I would bounce back, it was nothing short of miraculous EVERY TIME! I astounded the doctors and still do to this day.

When I would go for my follow-up appointment a week after my hospital discharge, they would say they couldn't believe their eyes. Furthermore, after performing my lab work-ups to check my blood counts, they were further amazed at how rapidly I had recovered. I remember Mrs. Iola Williams, one of the practitioners at the sickle cell clinic of Children's Hospital in Washington, DC, would always say to me, "Chil', you are a walking miracle. You have one of the worst cases of this disease I've ever seen, yet when I see you outside of that bed, you don't look like a thing wrong with you. If I didn't know better, I wouldn't believe the hype." To that I would say, "Who else but God!"

CHAPTER 7

Family and Friends

WHEN YOU'RE DEALING with an illness, it's good to have friends and family as your foundation for a strong support system. I believe it does make a difference when it comes to your recovery as well as how you're able to cope with your disease. I am fortunate to have a fairly strong support system, of which my mother and grandmother have been the backbone and the main ingredients. It was through their efforts I was able to get through a lot of tough times. There were more than plenty of times when I didn't have the strength to fight; they fought for me, and the times I got discouraged and felt I just couldn't go on, they were there to hold me up and get me going again. There were many times I got so tired of going through it all, times I didn't have the strength to keep going, and times I would get frustrated with this disease, with myself, with the damn doctors and hospitals, and just the whole endless rigmarole. They were always there, overflowing with encouragement and love.

I love that my mother and grandmother were always there for me, but the only thing that irritated me was that as soon as I got sick or they knew I was sick, they would get on the horn, and the next thing you knew, the whole world would know my business. This disease is not a pleasant thing, and to piggyback that, I am a very private person. They were always telling everyone I was in the hospital, and I had all these strangers ringing my phone in the hospital when I was supposed to be sick and trying to get my rest. How irritating, but that was just them, Mommy and Big Mommy, and how they were.

When I'm going through my metamorphosis, as I like to and often call my crisis, I don't like just anyone knowing what is going on. Unless they are directly involved, like they were in my presence when I went into crisis or they were the ones that took me to the hospital. Other than that, I don't feel like it's any of their concern. My grandmother and mother, on the other hand, beg to differ. They would announce my hospitalization to anyone willing to listen; I'm talking milkman, postman, dog walker—you name it, they're privy. "That's the culture," my mother would often say, referring to the African culture, birthplace of the old adage "It takes a village to raise a child."

Talk about culture clash, try being a Liberian living in a completely different African environment at home as compared to the American Children's Hospital environment, then imagine Big Mommy on a bright sunny day, strolling in my room, bringing her stinking cow-foot soup in a plastic bowl for me at the hospital. How embarrassing.

It's not that I want to keep my hospitalization this big clubhouse secret. It's just that I have learned the hard way the games of the grapevine. You know them, especially the one I like to call the telephone game, where if you line five people side by side and whisper something in the first person's ear and tell them to tell the person next to them and so on, by the time the story gets to the last person, you end up with not only a totally different story from the one you told caller no. 1—it is absolutely inaccurate with plenty of embellishments or outright lies. That is always what happens when these two women play "telephone." The people I am most concerned about experiencing the backlash of this game are my younger brothers and sisters who are away at college and live in different far-off states and definitely don't need ANY added stress. They can only go by what they're told over the telephone; because of the distance, they cannot visit and see for themselves what's really going on with me.

Then there are the other family members. Now they're family, so of course they care about you, but more in that pitying sort of way, like, you know, "That po', po' child, you know—they say she ain't gon' have much of a life the way that 'thing' don' gripped her like it has." Oh yeah, my "family"—the distant ones, that is—they talk about me and they gossip, even though I'm sure they mean well. However, their stressful involvement in my life does not help matters. Realistically, I know they can pity me all they want; I refuse to fit neatly into anyone's little box. I have too many dreams, and I have my own plans, and most importantly, God has a plan for me and it's proven to be far beyond anyone's expectations.

My friends, in the same sense, go both ways at well. The ones who are not very close to me at all, they are the "pitiers." They may see me every now and then and probably talk to me even less, but let them hear through the grapevine I'm in the hospital, and there they come with their pity faces and "oh, how sad" expressions at the mention of my problem. Their reactions to me and my illness, many times, make me feel like "the poor invalid girl." Even though I know they aren't trying to make me feel that way on purpose, I still feel defensive and defiant toward them and their attitudes.

Most family members and friends act like I'm fragile or something, that I am so helpless I can't do this or that. It is annoying and hurtful to me because it's like they have every predisposed limitation in the book on me, ignoring my actual life's track record and what I know and have told them I am capable of doing.

My Dad

It was shortly after 2:00 a.m. when the (dreaded) ring of the telephone woke me out of an already troubled sleep. I would not have been scared to death with uncertainty if I didn't have a father fighting for his life in the ICU of Crawford Long Memorial Hospital. Unfortunately, I couldn't say the same for the rest of my family—my mom, aunts, uncles, and all of them were camped out on the living room floor in the private slumber party of hope. Everyone, the five of us, raced around for various items of clothing to throw on so that the caravan could finally get going in a mad dash to the hospital. It was unanimously decided that my uncle would stay behind to look after the kids—my younger sisters and brothers who were all still asleep. I was the oldest of the bunch, though not by much, but God forbid should they try to make me stay at home.

I was far from tired, but my body dragged along as though laden with fatigue. The car remained silent on the entire twenty minutes' ride to the hospital, each of us was lost in our own private thoughts, each with our varying degrees of fear illustrated on our faces, but each, no doubt, dreading the same devastating outcome and possibilities.

The wannabe sterile gray-and-white linoleum-tiled hallway, lined with ornamental directional signs and framed faux Monet pharmaceutical print ads reeled of a cocktail of watered-down urine, generic disinfectant, and disease. At the end of that hall, stationed in the second to the last room on the left, room 407, lay my father in the end stages of kidney cancer. The walk to his room felt like the walk down my own green mile. Little did I know what awaited me in the second to last room on the left at the end of that lonesome hallway. If I'd had a clue, I would never have made it past the elevators.

While my mom and aunts raced down the deserted corridor, a wave heavy of foreboding weighted down my feet like cement blocks. My legs felt like they had been on a journey of a thousand miles and couldn't go any further. "Come on here, Syd!" my mother said sharply, jolting me out of my self-imposed trance.

After what seemed like an eternity, I finally made it to the room. As I entered into the doorway of his room, I nearly fainted from the shocking scene that lay before me, as my mother and aunts rushed to my dad's side, showering him with kisses and hugs.

I turned and readied myself to run off in the other direction. The man lying in that bed in front of me could not possibly be my daddy. I tried unsuccessfully to regain my composure and keep my emotions in check as I took in the frightfully horrible sight that lay before me but still could not believe my eyes.

Like I said, this frail skeletal frame of a person was not my father. I absolutely refused to believe that or even accept that. I took in the vision of a man that couldn't have been more than 130 pounds at best. His frame was literally skeletal—I mean, he seemed to have only skin covering frail bones. He was so tiny, skinny. His hair—or should I say what was left of it—was matted and completely white in some spots as though he'd aged a good twenty, thirty years, and what hair wasn't matted down was completely gone. His skeletal frame was augmented by an extremely bloated torso. His stomach looked as though someone had inflated it with a helium pump or like he was nine months pregnant and due any day.

As everyone present in the room gestured for me to go closer, I remained statuesque as though an artifact in the Smithsonian. Mt feet were firmly planted midway between the doorway and his bed, and as if having a mind of their own, they absolutely refused to move. Not that I was objecting or trying very hard to coerce them otherwise even after I realized how stupid I looked, awkwardly planted in the middle of the room after everyone else had managed to find a seat or at least somewhere to fit in.

By now, my mother was sitting on one side of Daddy's bed, and my stepmother was on the other. My aunt Bendu had taken her place in a chair right next to the bed, and my other aunt, Alyce, who was at the foot of his bed, extended her hand in my direction, as if to draw me closer within the little semicircle they'd all formed around his bed.

I slowly relented and found my hand reaching out for her outstretched hand and silent invitation. As if on cue, she raised from her seat, prompting me to take her place. Still plagued with reluctance, I sat down on his bed and fearfully took his now tiny hands in mine in an attempt to be comforting.

But how could I possibly be comforting to this stranger? I didn't know this mere skeleton of a man that lay before me, and he was certainly not my father. Not the father I knew and loved more than my own life. Big Jim, my daddy, was 6'5", 250 pounds of nothing but muscle. His body was fit and chiseled like that of a professional bodybuilder. His hands were so huge I could fit both of mine into one of his, even with the cancer, which he had contracted less than four months prior.

I still could not believe it. How does a man, virtually in a fairly normal state less than a week prior, end up in this state, basically looking like the Crypt Keeper from *Tales of the Crypt*, after walking—and I do emphasize *walking*—into a hospital for a mere check-up a few days ago and now has ended up in this fragile state, literally at death's door? A check-up? Days! Good God!

Guys

I never divulge my Morpher secret right away and will only do so if I deem your character to be understanding, compassionate, genuine, and able to handle it. I have to get to know you well enough to trust you, swearing you to secrecy upon telling you about the Morpher.

This is important to me because although I am not ashamed of my disease, I do not want a whole lot of people knowing unless they have to (strictly on a need-to-know basis), simply because some people cannot handle that kind of information either because of ignorance or being faint-spirited. I actually had a guy I was casually dating for probably about a month or two ask me if it was CONTAGIOUS. I mean, how ignorant can you be!

Also, the Morpher is not the easiest thing to introduce to new people, and it can be difficult to explain the ins and outs and dos and don'ts of what I go through or what happens with the metamorphosis at the onset of an episode. It seems so hard for people who have had no exposure and know nothing about the disease to actually comprehend what I go through. The whys, hows, and whats happen to me.

The good ones have taken good care of me, and that's not an easy job because I'm very impatient when I am sick. I try to be very self-sufficient, not asking for help with anything unless it is absolutely necessary. I don't like them seeing me when I am sick. I always think they're going to look at me differently.

Oh my goodness, I have had some embarrassing instances with guys and their crash course in Sickle Cell with Sydney 101! It makes me shudder just to think of some of the occasions when I had gotten sick and had some of my worst crises in the presence of my male companions over the years. Especially when I was younger—I mean it is bad enough when you're going through your teenage years—well, actually, from sixteen on up, which is when I started openly dating guys. I stress *openly* because prior to that, I would have a few boyfriends or talk to guys here and there but on the low, so my mother wouldn't find out.

My first real steady boyfriend was Nathan. Oh my gracious, that boy was hella fine, and I CANNOT stress that enough! He was a medium-build, somewhat muscular, six-foot-three hunk of a guy. He was mixed (Caucasian and African American). I guess the politically correct term would be *mulatto*, although I absolutely hate using that term. He had beautiful blue-green eyes and medium- to light-brown hair, nice teeth, the whole nine.

At the time we met in August, I was only a few months shy of my sixteenth birthday, but he had already graduated from high school earlier that June. We started dating shortly after the last semester of my sophomore year in high school. I guess at the time we were going out, he was about eighteen or nineteen, because he was about two years older than me.

We met at the Cuckoo's Nest, which was actually a restaurant, but they would host sixteen to twenty-one parties from 9:00 p.m. to 1:00 a.m. on Sunday nights before a holiday when we didn't have to go to school the next day. It was an underage hangout spot that was kinda like a club (nightclub, not recreational club) that used to be open in Olney, Maryland, way back in the day. That spot stayed packed in the summer and on holidays.

Nathan and I had the best year of my whole high school existence that year. We did just about everything together. He had just bought himself a new car the previous summer, so he would pick me up from school just about every day. I didn't know what riding the bus was that year. I was definitely the cat's meow, as I am every year, but this year I had the guy EVERY GIRL WANTED. I had broads hatin' me left and right, everywhere we went. We were so inseparable it got to the point whenever one of us was out without the other, everyone would be like "Where's Sydney?" or "Where's Nathan?" It was pretty ridiculous. For the longest time, we had the best relationship. We would always double-date with either my friends or his friends, and for a time, we managed to hook his cousin Joe, whom he was very close with, up with one of my girlfriends Christa, so we would double with them.

For spring break that year, we decided to go to Ocean City for the week, so we rented a fully furnished two-bedroom-and-two-bath condo for the six of us. It was Nathan and I; his best friend, Jermaine; his girlfriend, Shaniece; and Joe and his girlfriend, Jessica. We began planning months in advance, so we were able to get the condo, which was in a high-rise directly overlooking the beach for a really great price. I think each of us only had to come up with one hundred and sixty dollars for the rental plus twenty-five bucks a piece for groceries. What a blast we had. That turned out to truly be one of the best vacations, let alone spring breaks I've ever had—EVER!

Nathan and I had so much fun we decided to go back to Ocean City later that summer—I guess to recapture the wonderful time we had on our previous trip, which turned out to be a big mistake. First off, because it was kind of a last-minute trip—we couldn't find anyone to go with us—all our friends had summer jobs and couldn't get away on such short notice, or they just didn't have the dough or desire to go to Ocean City. Well, we decided to go anyway, just the two of us. We figured, how bad could it really be to get a hotel in the middle of summer—mind you, without prebooking reservations. So we hopped on the road to take a last-minute road trip, and off we went. Nathan picked me up around 10:00 a.m. that Friday morning, and we got on the road to OC. I can't even begin to remember where my mother thought I was going, but you can rest assured it wasn't two-hundred-plus miles away to Ocean City—me being sixteen, with my nineteen-year-old boyfriend. She would've had two fits—one for my benefit and one for his! I can just imagine what her reaction would have been if I had told her. I must have told her I was spending the weekend at one of my girlfriend's houses or something like that. The drive was fairly uneventful—boring actually—I was just happy to be with my man for the long weekend. We couldn't wait to get there and have some real fun. I guess we were really just trying to recapture the time we had with our friends on the last trip. We were trying a little too hard, now that I look back in hindsight. You really can't live a moment twice—or anything for that matter.

Nathan never really had to take me to the hospital, being that I was in high school and lived at home with my mother, who did all that. The only time he did take me was when we were playing basketball and I fell on my foot and broke it, but that did not count.

I did make various hospital trips with Daniel. Right after I met him, like the next day or something, I went into the hospital, and I didn't end up calling him until about a week later. I thought he'd forgotten about me by then, and he'd thought the same about me.

"THE MORPHER"

I didn't tell him I had been in the hospital but that I had been out of town. I was such a liar!

One night, I got sick right after Daniel and I went fishing down in Fort Washington Park. We had to get the boat back on shore, so we carried it, and I helped, and I think that's probably what precipitated the Morpher. I couldn't get out of the car when we got to his parents' house, just a five-minute drive up the road. We left his parents' house and went back to my place, and I collapsed on the floor as soon as I got inside the door and could not move thereafter. He was truly out of his element and totally bewildered. It was written all over his face. He was scared to go to the CVS to pick up some over-the-counter pain medicine. I think that was when I started using large dosages of over-the-counter pain meds in substitution for my prescription meds when I did not have any, which was more often than not. When he got back and gave them to me, he lay on the floor beside me and held me until I fell asleep. That was so sweet. He could definitely be sweet and wonderful when he wasn't out whoring, but that's a whole 'nother book.

Dan always stayed with me, whether he had to go to work or not, unlike the others who would never miss work to stay with me, come to think of it, except for once or twice. There were a few times Dan took me to Georgetown University hospital, where, it turned out, his mom worked. After Dan and I broke up, I never wanted to and refused to go there unless it was absolutely necessary, for fear of running into her.

Andre, he did take me to the hospital once when we were out late together, and it started out of the blue—or was it when we were just hanging together? No, it was in my own apartment at Northgate, and I called him in the middle of the night, and he took me to Holy Cross Hospital in Silver Spring. He stayed with me all night and into the morning even though he had to go to work.

I remembered the first time I got sick during or immediately following intimacy was with David. After that, it would happen somewhat frequently. I started being afraid of having sex because I would usually get sick. For the more ignorant ones, when that occurred, they probably really thought it was CONTAGIOUS!

CHAPTER 8

Stress

Catch-22 (Starting Over)

S TRESS IS ONE of my biggest problems. It's funny how stress works in my life. I often find myself caught up in a catch-22 situation. It's goes something like this: I am an achiever. I have always been an achiever, and more likely than not, I always will be. When I am unable to achieve, or am delayed or prevented from achieving, I begin to go into this major panic-riddled tailspin. I start feeling inadequate, unsuccessful, and lacking, and a generally deep feeling of failure begins to plague my spirit. The times that this has often occurred are usually after I have been bedridden or hospitalized for a lengthy period of time.

Of course, one might say, "Well, you're sick, you're not supposed to be doing anything except resting and recuperating." That's all well and good for most; however, that does not cut it for me. I don't know why, but it never has. I guess I can attribute that to my overly high expectations of myself. Mentally, a week seems adequate enough time to recover from one of my frequent bouts; however, more often than not, my body, physically, rarely concurs. But all who have befriended stress often and intimately enough know that it begins in the mind, picking at you mentally; at least that's where it starts with me.

Here's about where the catch-22 begins. See, most times when I become ill suddenly and wind up being down for the count for weeks at a time, I usually end up losing what seem to be the things that are most important in my life, like employment, friends, social status, and anything else I have actively going at that particular time. You might say to yourself, how can you lose all that just from being in the hospital for a few weeks, a couple of months, or whatever?

For me, it unravels like this: I'm good; I'm working, hanging out, dating, or probably have a man stashed away somewhere, everything summating to what appears to be a normal everyday life. Then boom, out of the blue—I mean literally out of nowhere—I'll go into a major crisis, wind up in the hospital, with no possibility of parole for the next seven to ten—days, that is—and, more often than not, two or three times as long as that.

First domino—there goes my job. I've painfully learned from experience that no matter how understanding an employer and people on the job may claim and even appear to be, their empathy is usually very short-lived, especially in terms of someone with a debilitating or reoccurring health problem.

Each time I go into the hospital for a period of time, I feel like I'm starting my life all over again from scratch, anew! Employers would dismiss me and treat me like I was nothing—EXPENDABLE. A few have even sent me grand bouquets of flowers along with their pink termination slip to my hospital bed.

Starting over seems to be the story of my life. Most people think of starting over as a good thing, a fresh start with a new job, a clean slate with new people, the beginning of a new life. That's all well and good, fine and dandy and all, but try doing that every couple of months, just about every single year of your life. It's not pretty. It's tiresome. Hell, it's downright exhausting, and it gets old real quick!

CHAPTER 9

Health Care

Doctors

IT MAKES ME angry that here we are in the twenty-first century, a whole new millennium, in the heights of technology where we've been able to visit Mars, clone fetuses, make promising strides in stem cell research, and yet there are physicians out there—or so they call themselves—who don't know anything about sickle cell anemia. How is that possible, pray tell? I mean, what exactly are these morons being taught in medical school? That's almost like learning to read and write but being absent the day they taught punctuation.

Okay, so I'm overdramatizing. But it does make me wonder how it is possible. Yes, I'm well aware that sickle cell disease is not on the top of the list when it comes to critical ailments—to me, for sure, but not to others. However, it is relevant, it is real, and therefore should have some priority in the medical curriculum. I guess it is along the same lines as how, in the American school system, we spend a great deal of time learning about American history, how Christopher Columbus discovered America, who invented what and when, but in the majority of these same history books and in the majority of the curricula, there is probably all of one page about African American history and the roles blacks played in the development of this country.

Doctors are strange and funny people. Not funny "ha ha" but funny as I don't quite get them—their MO, modus operandi, if you will. The science of medicine, in my opinion, is one of, if not *the* most significant and imperative field in all existence. My mother used to say to me all the time, "Without health, there is nothing, you can have nothing." At the time I did not appreciate the depth of that statement. But truly, everything is based on health. You cannot be anything or anyone, from a successful businesswoman to the most downtrodden bum on the street, without health. There is no accomplishment without health. Everything starts and ends with health, when you really think about it. You get my point!

Now physicians are these respected persons who have chosen to dedicate their lives essentially to the pursuit of health by thoroughly mastering the human body. What the body is comprised of, its functionality, and its responses to various situations, stimuli, etc. For years and years, they've studied this complex entity and its conditions—in short, health. How to achieve, maintain, retain, and sustain HEALTH and on and on and on. Now what amazes me in light of all this is when someone—I for instance—goes to these said professionals, say, for the first time (they've never met me, don't know me from Adam, keeping in mind that like a fingerprint, God made each and every one of us affordably similar yet substantially different), they will proceed with a "wham, bam, and thank you, ma'am" act.

At least the ones I have encountered will sit in a room with me for maybe roughly nine minutes, give or take an extra five minutes or so (and I'm being quite generous, mind you), and sum up the entire diagnosis and treatment and add in a "Have a nice day" while claiming to have summarized my medical problems. In all my many, many, many—and add some more to that—instances of being treated by physicians, that is the one thing that absolutely amazes me and galls me about these societal geniuses. I'm like, "How on earth do these yahoos get away with this nonsense? Am I the only one that is so utterly appalled? I mean, really!"

Health care, today, is one of the most booming industries. Honestly, they've got all kinds of rackets out there. Don't even get me started on this whole horse-and-buggy scam this country peddles to the most needy of its citizens, called insurance. But I digress. These doctors—now I know my reference sounds exceedingly and biasedly broad, however, for good reason.

Sad to say, the majority of physicians and other health-care providers do, in fact, practice this "get 'em in, get 'em out," grab-and-dash style of medicine that they call patient care, in which neither patience nor care is really administered. I'm sorry, but

SYDATU HOLDER

a doctor's appointment that is comprised of a forty-five minute wait in a well-manicured with all the frills and thrills reception area then a twenty-minute poke session with what you hope is a licensed phlebotomist (whom you pray washed her hands before coming to draw your blood) using your arm like a pin cushion and finally ending with a six-minute bull crap meet-greet-assess-and-treat small talk gibberish sit-down session with the actual doctor, who insists on finishing your sentences in order to shut you up and get you out the door a little quicker. That is *not* what I call *patient care*!

In all my years of more than frequent cohabitation in this bizarre world, I have yet to see even one doctor whose care I was under veer away from this MO and do otherwise. Trust me, I'm ready and waitin' for just one to prove me wrong, make me eat my words—something, anything—I'll be happy to. Not! At least not to date, anyway.

Hospitals

I remember one instance about ten years ago, when I was living in the heart of Washington, DC, not too far from my old alma mater, Howard University, which of course equates to hardly one of the better neighborhoods in the city, I was sick and alone and made the mistake of calling for an ambulance to take me to the hospital. This, of course, was before I became a veteran player in the brutal politics of inner-city hospital hopping alone. I was still wet behind the ears—fresh out of the comfort and protection of Children's Hospital and with "still a minor" status. Now I am older and, most importantly, a jaded by-product of the abusive health-care system.

BIG MISTAKE—for several very pertinent reasons, starting with the first catch—the ambulance doesn't and is not required, by law or otherwise, to take you to the best hospital, just the closest. So off I went to one of the worst hospitals in the entire city. I won't repay their injustice by revealing the name for corroboration, but believe me, it was BAD! And the crappy thing about the whole episode is that I really, really didn't want to call an ambulance. I mean I contemplated and went back and forth with the idea for a good part of an hour or so.

My dilemma being first, I'm a very private person, especially when it comes to my health situation, and nothing draws attention more than a siren and flashing lights, paramedics storming the residence, and dragging you out on a stretcher. Talk about nosy nellies! You'll be the topic of conversation on the block for months to come, and the rumor mill will be out of control.

I heard later, from one of my "well-intentioned" neighbors, not long after that episode, that the word around the building had been that I'd flatlined in the elevator and the paramedics had miraculously revived me between the sixth and second floors—I lived on the tenth floor! When she told me this, my first thought was to smack her for being so stupid, give my thirty-day notice, and post a note on the bulletin board, by the mailboxes, that not only were they all profoundly mistaken but also that they all needed to mind their own damn business or I'd be forced to disclose that apartment 1001 was sleeping with 305 and that 907 had trashed the door of 904 because they wouldn't turn the music down—but I digress.

What could I do? The pain I was experiencing was becoming more unbearable by the minute. I relented, dialed 911, and tried to find relief in the thought that I would soon be in the haven of the emergency room, with relief in sight. I needed to get dressed and get ready for the difficult ride. It seemed to take forever; it felt like it took an hour just to get my pants on, though it was actually just five minutes—for each leg, that is.

Upon arrival at the hospital, I was deposited in a bay and forgotten. Waiting patiently and calling out gently didn't work, so I banged on the walls to get the attention of any medical staff. I was made to wait three hours before being seen. By that time, my pain was way out of control when I was requested to give urine samples and take x-rays, which meant getting up and going to the bathroom and radiology, all before getting anything for pain management.

Yeah right! I used to go for that before—do all that moving around, trying my best to do what was requested of me, thinking it would help me receive treatment quicker and more proficiently . . . NOT! Now I don't get up or move around to do anything until I am first given some type of pain relief. I tell them exactly that too because when I do go through all that moving around, which aggravates the pain even further, the level of degree and intensity kicks up a good ten times. Besides all that, I still have to wait another lengthy period before receiving anything for the pain.

It's like they just don't get it! So forget it! Forget them! I finally got out of the bed and went home without having gotten any medical attention, or any attention at all—forget about *medical*. When I got home, I took twenty Tylenol PMs. I figured I'd either get some relief or die, either of which would be better than the pain I was in. However, by the next day, I had gotten worse and went to another "white" hospital. Only this time I took a cab. It still took about an hour to be taken back to the treatment area and to a bed. This time I could not afford not to stay; I couldn't walk.

The Mad Lab

I think I can honestly say the worst doctor or hospital experience I ever had, hands down, had to have been my brief stay at a general hospital, or the "mad lab," as I'd like to think of it.

The doctor walked in arrogantly, came over to my bedside with his face laden with skepticism, looking me over as though I were common curbside trash. He looked as though he'd already come to a conclusion of my diagnosis prior to my uttering a word. He appeared resentful that he had to take time out of his schedule to be bothered with the likes of me. If I told you I remembered his name, I'd be lying. For me, it was not worth the nano space to retain his name, credentials, or any other informational statistics, although I will never forget the encounter.

"So what seems to be the problem, or are you just here for a drug fix?" he muttered. I couldn't believe what I was hearing. Was this complete jerk actually a board-certified practicing physician or some horrendous comic-relief reject? Drug fix! If I weren't in so much pain, I would have not only given him a piece of my mind, explicit excerpts and all. I would have probably hauled off and slapped him, overlooking the eminent possibility of landing an assault charge. But with my body riddled with pain from head to toe, all I could manage to muster was a threatening, acid-spewing scold shot dead in his direction. "I'm having a severe sickle cell crisis, with pain in my lower back, both legs, both elbows, and my chest," I loudly whispered, barely able to choke the words past my clenched teeth.

As I lay helplessly gasping, wriggling in pain, he looked me over once again, this time much like his initial survey—unenthusiastically, as if he were witnessing paint drying. "Have you been here before, Ms. Holder?" he bellowed. "We get a lot of you in here looking to get a quick high," he said, adding insult to injury.

First of all, exactly who were the *you* he was ignorantly grouping me in with? Secondly, was he purposely trying to antagonize me, or was he really that clueless, stupid, and naive because any half-wit idiot with some common sense (forget about street smarts) putting two and two together would know that if all I wanted to do was get high, the hospital would be the last place any feigner would go. Why pay eight-hundred-plus dollars to lie in a hard, uncomfortable plastic cot with a poly-foam mattress two-thirds the size of a twin bed in the middle of a disease-infested, loud, and peace-jarring emergency room that reeks of what smells like a sterile cocktail consisting of urine with a twist of disinfectant? In addition, why pay the inflated market rate of one meperdine, Dilaudid, or morphine shot at $100–150 a pop, which is only about the standard 4 mg morphine or 75 mg Demerol, when you can get it at one fourth of that price and none of the hassle on the street from the your everyday, garden-variety, urban-street pharmacist, the corner dealer? I mean really, let's cut the crap! Was this joker for real?

To add insult to injury, he was a fellow African—not that that would have allowed any vindication, but his ignorant behavior is what I would more quickly expect from a Caucasian, who, more than likely, was bound to be oblivious to this sort of segregated, uncommon illness and its characteristics.

It turned out to be a twenty-four-hour nightmare before I was actually admitted, and I shared a room with five other patients, where they had us flanked together like cattle.

I was left crying for hours. I banged on the walls with my water pitcher, attempting to get the nurse's attention for assistance. During that time, another patient, a man with a knife, was threatening to stab a nurse. Based on similar actions of the other patients, that seemed to be the universal call bell of choice for any viable human attention.

Can we say "need more pain medication"? One initial shot was not meant to last eight hours, especially to effectively battle a pain intensity of 10 out of 10 on the rector scale.

No one knew where I was. I finally tracked down my mom by calling all around and getting my uncle Jimmy to get an SOS message to her begging her to help get me out of that hospital. Uncle Jimmy came and picked me up around six or seven the next evening.

My clothes had been stolen. Needless to say, I disconnected my IV myself and hightailed it out of there AMA (against medical advice) in my hospital gown with me trying half successfully to keep my rear end under wraps. Sneaking away to a better, plusher hospital, if there is such a thing.

CHAPTER 10

I'm Tired of It All

A S IF THAT wasn't enough, let me regale another incident that proved utterly UNACCEPTABLE! Same location less than a year later. To be precise, three hours—that's how long it took for them to acknowledge me, only this time it was after I had been admitted and transported to the oncology unit upstairs. Three hours of lying in agonizing pain, waiting to be tended to, cared for, or given any indication that as a person, I mattered.

In the beginning of April, two o'clock in the morning, I was awakened from sleep, gripped with merciless pain. The same pain that exerts itself in the same obtrusive manner, descending upon my entire body systematically, as if for roll call—beginning in my back and then traveling within a matter of minutes to both my legs and then my arms, time after time after time again. It was the most severe attack I'd had in a while—about three months—and it gripped me—I wouldn't say *unexpectedly* per se, but I didn't have enough pain medication to counter the attack.

I had been having "mini" controllable crises over the course of the previous week, but I had been able to reign "the beast" back in by quickly taking medication at the very onset and being still so that by the next morning the pain had subsided considerably. I even called my doctor to refill my prescription because I had the feeling I would not make it to my scheduled appointment at the end of that week. The problem was that the freakin' PA, Leslie, wrote the prescription for twenty tablets.

Twenty tablets—what the heck was I supposed to do with twenty pills? I took the pills in quantities of five to six at a time. I don't know what she was thinking. Thus, I ended up running out of the medication two days after I got the prescription. Nice, right? My foreboding, added to the significant amount of stress

I was under, didn't make for a good preemptive strike at all. As a matter of fact, I was sure it advanced the impending attack.

By 3:00 a.m., the pain was off the hook. Although I didn't want to, I knew I would have to make a trip to XYZ Hospital.

So I was lying there, dreading the fact that I would inevitably have to make a trip to that hospital again and there was just no way around it, but I was procrastinating until the very last minute. All because I knew the headache that awaited me.

So what's the point? At the end of the day, when it's all said and done, what does it all really matter? I ask myself this question all the time.

Most recently, I've come to a point in my life where I feel like I am literally on my last leg. My body has withheld so many years of wear and tear it has become painfully apparent to me that at the rate I am going, if things don't change soon, I won't last much longer. It was at this time I decided I would once again try this proactive stuff, taking the initiative to consistently and actively try to stay two steps ahead of this monster instead of simply riding its back.

My disease is one of minimal complication. It is what it is. In fact, I think it's the seemingly simplicity of it that, at times, deems it so frustrating. I get stressed, I get a crisis. I don't get enough rest, I get a crisis. I catch a cold, a urinary tract infection, or any other type of infection, I get a crisis. Overexposure to cold or hot temperatures or any other injury that presents stress to my immune system, all will materialize into a full-bloom crisis. These are simple factors, yet for me they can be fatal.

When I go into a crisis, the only remedy is pain medication, antibiotics to fight off precipitating infection, and blood transfusion to bring my red blood cell count up to a reasonably stable level, and that's about it.

The doctors tell you to drink plenty of fluids, get lots of rest, don't overexert yourself, and try to limit the stress in your life. Simple, right? Like explaining how to take cough medicine when you have a cold.

But all these factors fall under *if, might, in case,* and *maybe.* Ever try juggling in a three-ring circus? I rest my case!

Anyway, like I was saying, recently, I came to a point where I decided to be proactive, or more proactive, for the umpteenth time. I'd just gotten a new doctor, who seemed like a really good guy, with good, caring, and honest intentions. I figured it would be like starting over with a clean slate. He wouldn't have any prejudices, preconceived notions, or biases when it came to my care.

In the new testament of the Bible, Jesus says you can't put new wine into old wine skin. I needed a new attitude, a renewed measure of faith and trust in my medical caregiver, and that is what I decided to commit to.

Now I don't know what it was about this particular doctor; he just gave me a good feeling when I first met him in the hospital. Anyone who knows me, knows that's rare, because after all I've been through with this disease, considering all the doctors and health-care professionals I've seen come and go, I can't say I hold a very high opinion of any of them. I can sniff the flukes out like a narcotics K-9 at the Mexican–American border. I've switched doctors several times in the past, either due to geographical convenience or just looking for someone who knew a little more or could care for me a little better than the last joker (doctor).

I can honestly say none has given me a sense of comfort as to their sincere efforts regarding my well-being. The last doctor I just disposed of—we'll call her Dr. X—made it clear she didn't give a rat's ass about me in any shape or form.

Most of them will at least try to play it off. Granted, in all honesty, I may not be the best patient, but who would be when you're constantly being told, "Well, Ms. Holder, you know the prognosis and what the outcome is of your disease. It's unfortunate you will not have longevity and maybe not much quality, but that is the harsh reality of this disease." Talk about cold, heartless jerk-offs. Could you at least try to crack a smile, look empathetic when speaking to me about the life (or lack of) I have to look forward to? God forbid you should try to smooth it out with a little warmth!

I've been fortunate to have a few good doctors that really cared, but most didn't. Some doctors get upset because I don't follow up with consistent visits. I do not go regularly because I could not afford to—no medical insurance! I feel very guilty because I want their treatment, but many times, I don't even have enough money to make the copay. Because of this, most doctors believed I am not serious about my health care and that I am not doing everything I possibly could to keep my demon at bay.

Well, after all I've been going through, we both know the situation, so what's the point? I should just keep rolling in to satisfy their conscience by believing they are giving me good care, when in all honesty, all it really amounts to is me fattening their pockets with money I don't have nor can afford.

I'm tired; I'm so tired of it all.

CHAPTER 11

Employment

Can a Sista Get a Job?

MY WHOLE LIFE, I'd been under the impression that the formula to earn a decent living was "education plus skills plus experience plus an excellent work ethic equals a good job," at the very least. I found out fairly quickly that I was sadly mistaken! I had an education, I had abundance of skills, and throughout my college years, I had picked up a very impressive body of knowledge and experience pertinent in corporate America.

From the age of sixteen, unlike my friends and most other young adults I knew who inhabited minimum-wage city, staffing fast-food joints, I'd always worked in offices. I obtained administrative positions through temp agencies while I went to school and during summer and, sometimes, winter breaks. I could answer a ten-to-twenty-line switchboard and handle calls with the proficiency of a seasoned telemarketer. I could type sixty to seventy wpm (words per minute), and I'd worked in just about every industry from marketing and advertising, insurance, health care, public relations, county and state government consumer services, telecommunications (satellite, computer semiconductor manufacturers) to HR staffing and government contracting with the Department of Justice. You name it—I'd worked in or had some sort of related experience in a wide variety of fields.

And with my health situation as bad as it's been, I think I've accumulated enough knowledge and hands-on experience in medicine and health care that I could probably defer a year or two of medical school if I chose to pursue a future in that arena— *not*! At this point, my respect level for most physicians and the health-care system in general is equivalent to that of garbagemen or politicians. Then again, scratch that—at least garbagemen are honest.

Anyway, I have always been professional, punctual, personable, very charismatic, and most importantly, I've always been a very ambitious go-getter. I don't wait to be told what to do, nor do I solicit micromanagement. No, I am assertive and always take the initiative, from start to finish. I look the part, speak the part, and can nail the part in any interview, any day of the week, against the best of candidates. I am every employer's golden child, or so I thought. I'll never forget my first wake-up call that opened my eyes to what corporate America was really all about, and boy, was it a rude awakening.

I was fresh out of college, and I was excited! My first full-time job out in the real world, and I was ready to bring home the bacon. I'd interviewed with several different companies over a period of three to four weeks in July and was expecting a call back any day. The first week after my interviews came and passed, I was really cool, even a little cocky, because I knew I had done extremely well in all of them, so I was certain I'd definitely end up with something. The only flicker of doubt or hesitation that concerned me at that time was if I would get the job that I really wanted, especially in light of my medical history. So the second week came and passed, and I was still waiting for a call back, any call back . . . but nothing. Now patience has never been one of my virtues, and back then, I was worse because I didn't even attempt to act as though it was, like I do now. I was waiting, waiting, waiting, and still nothing; all the while, days were beginning to feel like weeks, and the weeks began to feel like months.

In pure panic-attack fashion, I began to replay the interviews I'd thought I'd had in the bag over and over in my mind, analyzing every frame of recollection with a microscope, questioning and second-guessing myself. It was moving into the second week of August, and my self-assurance was flappin' in the wind like a carefree sail, only I wasn't feeling the least bit carefree. I was in a full-fledged panic, and the employment classifieds once again became my full-time, all-the-time companions, and then it came . . . a call back. They wanted me to come in for a second interview with the vice president of human resources. I was ecstatic, mainly because the jerks had finally called me back, one of them at least.

However, glad as I was to finally be given an opportunity, I couldn't help feeling a little disappointed because the company that called back first was not the position I'd really hoped for. Although I contemplated holding out for a response from my first choice, I quickly woke up from that pipe dream. The fact of the matter was, I was broke. I'd been out of work for just about the entire summer, and I needed to make ends meet and quickly, so I agreed to go in for a second interview with the second-choice company.

I purposely arrived at their offices about twenty minutes earlier than agreed upon, knowing they'd stick me in a conference room somewhere by myself and have me waiting forever. My plan was to make good use of the wait time by reviewing and refreshing my memory on the company's information—their products and services, customer demographics, the names of most, if not all, of the department heads and the role I was expected to play on the team. *Thank goodness I had sense enough not to chuck the company booklet I was given on my first interview that would privy me to this wealth of information*, I thought to myself, my lips curving into a sly grin. This may not be the job I wanted, but I was about to blow their minds with everything I knew about their company. Oh, and yes, the charm, which had been turned on the moment I hit the double glass doors, was about to be kicked up ten notches. Now understand, there is a healthy difference between charm and outright brownnosing, which I totally frown upon personally, but today, taking into consideration my malnourished bank account, I had planned on flirting very dangerously with that line.

I got off the elevator at the top floor of the five-story glass building and walked confidently through the brightly lit lobby and in the waiting area of the suite. *How befitting*, I thought to myself, *I'm on my way to the top, literally and figuratively speaking*. I quickly glanced down, giving myself a final once-over. The tailored crème-colored pinstriped skirt suit I was wearing fitted me to a T. The skirt, which fell slightly above my knees, was short enough to complement my long brown-colored stocking-clad legs without looking skanky yet long enough to pull off the look of a very stylish young professional executive. The tailored seams of the suit jacket comfortably hugged my waist, falling an inch or two below the waist of the skirt. I smoothed the lapel of my jacket and walked confidently up to the oversized mahogany reception desk in the middle of the room. "Hi, my name is Sydney Holder, and I have a two o'clock appointment with Carol Benning," I said boldly, my words echoing throughout the large open space.

A mousy, undernourished-looking lady who looked to be in her mid-to-late thirties peered up at me from behind the large U-shaped counter that seemed to swallow her up. She picked up the receiver of the telephone and murmured unenthusiastically, "She here," before quickly hanging up. She was so inaudible I wondered if the person she called had even heard her—I know I barely did, and I was standing right in front of her. "Mrs. Benning will be with you shortly, Ms. Holder," the taut-faced brunette said in a less-than-welcoming tone. I guess I'd have an attitude and walk around mad all day too if I looked like her. The black-rimmed glasses she had on seemed to swallow her face, causing her to look like an Ugly Betty look-alike. She was so thin and tiny she seemed to get lost behind the huge reception desk.

All those chips stacked against her and she still refused to smile! Then again, maybe it was because she had no lips. No, really, she had no lips—a sea of lipstick but no lips! Kinda like Susan Lucci from *All My Children*, except Susan Lucci is beautiful, so she gets a pass on the no-lips thing. What the hell was she painting lipstick onto? She should have saved that money and invested in Botox injections to the lips or something. *Girl, MAC can't help you—you need collagen*, I thought to myself. Half of me wanted to say, "Honey, that painted-line-masquerading-as-your-lips thing you got going on is not a good look, and you might wanna think about taking a Weedwacker to that unibrow that's nested on your face so you won't resemble a Chia Pet. With all those strikes, it wouldn't hurt to crack a smile here and there either! After all, you're already not the prettiest egg in the basket, and please lose the black-rimmed Ugly Betty glasses—they're the worst!" Thank God for self-restraint! That broad needed a serious makeover—somebody call a reality show for crying out loud! But ignoring temptation, in an attempt to maintain some measure of decorum, I politely smiled and said nothing.

"If you'll follow me, please, you can have a seat in the conference room," she said as her small frame made its way from behind the large mahogany desk sectional. She was even tinier than she initially appeared to be, standing no more than five feet, give or take. Next to me, she looked like a Muppet. My five-feet-nine-inch frame devoured her stunted build effortlessly. She walked briskly past me as I stepped aside to allow her to take the lead. *Lord, forgive me for bad mouthing one of your children*, I prayed, *but dang, what is up with that dress?* I continued in my mind, as my eyes darted up and down her backside in complete awe, astounded by her audacity to wear the butt-ugly green-and-orange paisley dress she had on. *Did this woman get dressed in the dark this morning? Ugh!* I shook my head in total amazement. *Note to self . . . thank God for blessing me with good looks and a sense of style*, I humbly thought as I murmured, "Thank God and amen" under my breath. "Note number 2 to self—if I get this job, I need to either (1) become fast friends with this chick and pull her sleeve to some serious grooming and fashion tips, (2) secretly leave a copy of the latest issue of *Vogue* or *W* magazine in her office mailbox, or (3) stay as far away from her as possible—not that bad style sense is contagious, but dammit, just to be on the safe side," I mused. I'm as PC—politically correct—as the next person, but dang, something needed to be said to this chick from this chick. Hell, leave a Post-it on the screen of her computer, "You need a makeover—TODAY, lady!" You can't get more anonymous than that.

This broad was seriously distracting me from my grind and focus, which was to nail this job. Looking at her was not exactly the most alluring enticement or "come work here" red carpet they could've rolled out, but the money was. It was time to get my mind back in the game. I chose a seat in the middle of the conference room and delicately sat on the edge of one of the maroon leather chairs so as not to wrinkle my pristine Calvin Klein suit. *Damn, I look good in my digs, if I may say so myself! I'd definitely hire me*, I thought to myself. I eagerly pulled the company booklet out of my briefcase (yes, I was doing it way big with the briefcase) and began reading the areas of importance I'd previously highlighted. I was professional; I was prepared, and not only were they about to see my game face, they were about to KNOW my game was TIGHT!

Forty minutes later, the door of the conference room swung open and in walked a lady that could've passed for Hillary Rodham Clinton's twin. I'd never seen her before and had no idea who she was. She wore a fire-engine-red skirt suit that hugged her body somewhat awkwardly. With every step, you could hear a swishing serenade escaping from beneath her skirt as her hosed thighs rubbed together, which was odd because she was not a heavy woman. Her strawberry-blonde curls framed her face, stopping just beneath her earlobes. She looked to be in her late forties or early fifties and had soft baby-blue eyes, which contradicted the stern, pursed-lipped glare she was emitting. Right on her heels came Lauren, the younger lady I'd initially interviewed with. The pine-green skirt suit she had on didn't do much to flatter her appearance at all—not to mention, the two of them standing next to each other made me think of Christmas. Lauren was sweet, though, and it showed in her eyes. I can tell a kind soul when I see one, and I must say the difference between an unkind soul and a kind soul is worlds apart. They both greeted me politely as I rose from my seat to shake their hands.

"So you're Sydney," Carol said in a strong, commanding voice. "Lauren has told me some good things about you."

"It's a pleasure to finally meet you, Mrs. Benning. I too have learned some very impressive things about you and the accomplishments you've made within Noisuf Technologies during your seven-year tenure with the company." Yes, it was time to bring out my A game. This lady was at the top of her field and among the who's who in the semiconductor manufacturing industry.

"Is that so? Well, by all means, please enlighten me," she baited.

I continued, "NT is the leading manufacturer of silicon semiconductors in the US to date. The company was started back in 1957 by Cecil and William Noisuf and was originally based in Medford, Oregon, but later relocated to Redding, California, before settling here in Maryland in 1989. NT grossed $15.7 million in sales last year, highest in the company history and industry annual gross. Last year, your manufacturing department just revamped their Clean Cast Labs to include optimizing integration schemes to put dielectrics into production."

We played semiconductor knowledge table-tennis fashion over the next hour. This was definitely going above and beyond the call of duty. After all, it's not like I was applying for the CEO's position, but when I aim to put my best foot forward, I do just that, oftentimes leaving shoes too big to fill.

"Well, I must say, Sydney, I am extremely impressed! Obviously you've done your homework on NT and the semiconductor industry. Most of our executive-level candidates don't even bother to come prepared with the body of knowledge you have exhibited here today. What made you decide to come to the table so overly prepared, if I may ask?"

Was she serious! "Overly prepared"—she considered this overly prepared? I wanted to laugh. For one, I'd always done this level of research for every professional interview I'd ever had, dating back to when I used to apply for administrative positions back in high school. With all the strikes against me to begin with, I'd have been stupid or plain naive if I didn't always come with my A game. I was young, under the age of most candidates going for management or executive positions. I was African American, and strike three, I was a woman. It didn't get any more real than that! Unless of course I was a black man! Today's workforce, as PC—politically correct—as it claims to be, would like to convince us (Americans) that it is in a mad dash to hire minorities regardless of race, ethnicity, or gender for upper-level positions. Unfortunately—or however you want to look at the situation—with Affirmative Action blowing in the wind and seemingly no longer as mandatory as it used to be a while back, individuals such as myself, with a number of pre-existing strikes against us, need to do any- and everything themselves to gain the advantage. But that's just my personal insight on the matter, coming from someone with hands-on human resources experience who has been on both sides of the table as interviewer and interviewee.

"Simply stated, Carol, when I set out to do something, accomplish something, or take on any task, really, I always bring my A game. And if I'm not going to come with my A game, I feel there's no point in me coming at all."

"Sounds like you're just the kind of person we need on our team. I can't make any promises yet because we do still have a few candidates scheduled for interviews. But I really like you, Sydney, and I think you will do very well here at Noisuf Technologies," Carol said with a wide grin.

She jumps, she shoots, she scores! I thought to myself. I indeed brought my A game and now I was going home with the ring. "Woo-hoo! I'm back in business!" I wanted to scream. I was ready to talk turkey with these chickens. I'm talking salary . . . bring me the bacon.

CHAPTER 12

Addictions

"MY NAME IS Sydney and I am an addict." I feel like I should be making that admission upon entering some clinical rehab program. However, if the truth be known, admittedly I have yet to build up the courage to actually take that step. Sure, I'm not an addict in the conventional sense of the word, but I've come to the realization that I do, in fact, have a problem. But it's not the kind of addiction I've always been accused of throughout my life because of the hardcore narcotics I've needed to take when in a pain crisis. Don't get it twisted—I don't snort coke, I don't shoot up heroin (or anything else), and I don't suck on crack pipes for jollies. In fact, if I wanted to be cliché, I could certainly get away with saying I'm really not really any kind of addict because everyone does it—take an over-the-counter analgesic or sleep aid every now and then.

Yeah, I could get away with saying that, but it's high time I stopped ducking, dodging, and denying. And to think, all this time—my whole life, basically—I've had stupid idiot doctors accusing me left and right of faking my illness to get fixes of morphine, Demerol, or the like. Little did they know those heavy narcotic pain medications have never been my hang-up . . . NEVER! It's like I'm almost proud to say that, seeing the warped way I think of the whole "addiction" bit. I know lots of people who are addicted to these types of medications. A lot of them developing habits or addictions because of being treated for an illness or injury. As with everything else, I am different. The heavy narcotic meds like morphine, Demerol, etc., never really appealed to me, as strange as that may sound.

Over the years of constantly having to take heavy narcotics for real pain, I've built up such a tolerance that normal doses barely do anything for my pain when I am in a severe crisis. Let alone get me high. I don't like the way they make me feel so drained and disoriented.

There have been so many times when I've been sick and I progressed to the road to recovery but I couldn't remember anything about the first few days of my hospital stay. I mean nothing! I couldn't tell you what was done to me, who came to visit, or what happened. I often feel like I've lost huge chunks of my life because I just can't remember. It's a scary thing not knowing what people are doing to you in a place as open and unsecured as a hospital, more especially in my case, because I was, and still am, alone the majority of the time I go into the hospital. That's not the kind of high that is appealing to me. I sometimes sleep for days when I'm on these narcotic medications. Who wants to sleep for days, wake up, and not know up from down?

It's hard to pinpoint exactly when and how my dependency on over-the-counter analgesic began. Actually, I have a scope on how—or at least the events that transpired. It was only occasionally and without thought at first and then progressing consistently enough to become habitual. For a long time I did not believe I had a problem.

CHAPTER 13

The Pain Is Real

W E'VE ALL EXPERIENCED pain, real or imagined, in one form or another. The pain suffered from sickle cell is not only physical but also very much mental and emotional. For me, the physical pain, however awful and unbearable most of the time, is the least of the three. The mental anguish of wondering why I am like this and why I can't be normal usually creates the emotional depression. This depression pain is real.

I have had many things stripped away from me and many things that have made me feel obviously different because of this disease. This constant stripping is the main cause of my emotional and mental scars.

Oh, these scars—so many, all my life! Some go away and some don't.

The physical scars fade eventually. The emotional and mental scars of mistreatments result in depression and self-deprecations like "Why am I like this?" and "Why did this happen to me?" are deep and debilitating. Especially scars from family, friends, and people in general with their discounted attitude toward me, constantly insinuating "You're not good enough."

The mental and emotional pain of trying to obtain a livelihood and hold on to JOBS when you are physically challenged is indescribable. Corporate America is not kind to the sick, different, handicapped, or disabled, though we are just trying to earn a living like everyone else.

The irony of that is how, on the other hand, these same fellow Americans are always harping on how they don't want to have to support the welfare-hoarding, discounted, and disenchanted like me.

Which is it? Welfare with dignity, or physical, emotional, and mental PAIN!

Bet it was never looked at in that light!

CHAPTER 14

Beauty for Ashes

I T'S FUNNY, YOU know—all through this book I've
referred to sickle cell as "my disease," "my illness," "my
Morpher," and so on and so forth. Yes, it is very much all those
things. However, at this point in my life, after it's all been said
and done at thirty-three years old, I can now honestly say, "Yes,
I am a chronic sickler! No, it is not a pretty or good thing," but
in many ways, I owe who I am and what I have become—good,
bad, or indifferent—to my disease. I don't believe that I would
be the person I am today if I had not experienced all that I have
experienced. If I had not gone through the kind of pain I have
endured, I would not have had the strength and resilience that I
have. I don't believe that I would have had the do-or-die spirit that
burns within me.

For a lot of years, I walked around feeling sorry for myself and
the cards that I'd been dealt. I might as well have had "Why me!"
stamped on my forehead in fluorescent paint because whenever
I would get sick, that was the only thing I would wrap my mind
around. Whenever I looked at "normal" people living normal
lives, free of any burdens remotely similar to mine, that's where
my mind would go.

The majority of the people I know, and many in the world for
that matter, have never even been in a hospital, let alone occupied
it as their second home. To me that was astonishing. Here I was,
practically a permanent fixture in hospitals and doctors' offices for
the entire span of my existence, while there were millions of people
in this world that couldn't even relate to any of my experiences.
That was my mind-set—"Why me?"

When I was younger, I remembered many times I would come
home after spending weeks in the hospital, and I'd be so depressed
because I knew I had to start all over again. Rebuild my life and

set out to regain whatever it was that I'd lost or stripped away while I was absent from life—whether it be a job, a boyfriend, or grades when I was in school. I knew I would have to go out and take back whatever it was that I'd lost, and sometimes it was a lot. The whole cycle was so exhausting, but it was what I have had to do every time, and sometimes, I just wasn't up to it.

During the time when I was still living at home, my mother was my saving grace. She didn't allow me to sit around for days and weeks feeling sorry for myself. Usually, the first few days up to a week, she'd let me rest and get reacquainted with everyday life at home. But once she knew that I was fully recuperated, she would pull the shades up to penetrate the dark room (I always wallowed in a dark room, even in the middle of the day), open the windows, let fresh air in, and drag me out of the bed. She would scream, holler, fuss, and fight with me. "Get out of that bed and get back into life," she would always say. She knew my spirit had sunk and retreated into this deep pit of darkness, and she would fight with me tooth and nail to pull me out of it.

She would say, "I wouldn't make you if I didn't think you could do." For that I will eternally be grateful to her and thank God for her every day, although at the time I didn't like her very much for pushing me the way she did. She believed in me when I didn't believe in myself. She gave me courage when I had forgotten my own, and she gave me strength to push through when mine didn't measure up to the size of a mustard seed. I always tried to imagine what my life would be like if I didn't have the problem of living with chronic sickle cell disease. I would daydream and think of what a wonderful life I would've had. I imagined I'd be married, with beautiful healthy kids, and I'd have an incredible career, CEO of a Fortune 500 company, or have a lucrative, thriving business. I'd travel all over the world and undertake adventurous pastimes like skydiving. I dreamed of being successful, valued, and respected.

Seems like my whole life I've been waiting to die. I mean literally from as far back as I can remember—seven, eight years old. Most kids feel like they're going to live forever, yet there I was, seven years old, waiting on death. That was the monster living in my closet. Back then I was afraid, terrified that it'd swoon down on me before I could make it to my next birthday. The overachiever in me wanted to do everything in a hurry—live my entire life out and do all the things I ever wanted to do in a matter of weeks or months. I was in a race against time. It felt like my life was comprised of mile markers than anything else. First, I felt I wouldn't make it to age fifteen, then eighteen, twenty, twenty-five, and so on. I never saw myself well into adulthood. I figured maybe, if I were lucky, I'd get to my early thirties . . . tops. It was stressful! Not much changed except after I reached about twenty, I no longer feared death. Quite the opposite, actually. I began to welcome the Grim Reaper. In fact, my behavior, in every way, summoned him, daring him to descend upon me and relieve me of my life. I constantly dared him to put me out of my misery like a wounded animal. It's funny—I almost called this book *Living to Die.*

W hat I couldn't see then was that I AM VALUED, SUCCESSFUL, and RESPECTED and further, I CAN have the family and career and still do all those things I'd always longed to do. It took me a long time to get to this place. I call it freedom from self, because all this time I've been standing in my own way, bound by my own fears and insecurities. I still have a long journey in which to travel, but now, I am walking my road with hope and confidence.

For all this, I give God the glory because His grace and ONLY His grace enabled me to triumph despite painful circumstances and adversities. Only his love and more grace enabled me—sickly, inadequate, unemployable, financially liable beyond the greatest liability (by the world's standards anyway)—to soar. Only His grace allowed me to be, on many occasions, envied by my "normal" peers—for what or why, I don't know. For that reason, today, I can actually embrace my Morpher, disease, illness, or whatever label you want to put on it. I'm no longer embarrassed or ashamed. I no longer feel inadequate, insufficient, lacking, freakish, pathetic, or any of the other things I once felt or was made to feel by how others treated me. I know beyond a shadow of a doubt, like I know my own name, that I am truly blessed. I now know that not only does everything happen for a reason but that God, my heavenly father that I love and serve, does not make mistakes . . . EVER!

CHAPTER 15

God's Good Plan

I HAVE COME TO learn, become rooted, firmly believe, and can attest to the fact that God has a plan for my life. Moreover, the Word says He has a plan for each and every one of our lives and not just any plan but a GOOD plan. I also believe that each and every one of us has a distinct purpose for our lives, whether we know it or not and whether we believe it or not. I can remember, when I was younger, God putting this on my heart. I couldn't have been more than eleven or twelve years old, yet it was as real and as true to me as my own name, as though it was etched on my spirit at the time of my conception. There is a passage in the Bible that says, "When I was woven together in the depths of the earth your eyes saw my unformed body. All the days ordained for me were written in your book before one of them came to be" (Psalm 139:15–16).

I knew God had something great planned for my life. I don't know how I knew; I just did. It was innate. I remember being so excited when I received this bit of revelation. I ran downstairs and said to my mother, "Mom, God is going to do something big in my life! I don't know what it is yet, but it is going to be wonderful and huge and I'll be helping a lot of people!"

She just smiled and said, "That's nice, sweetie," and looked at me like I was from Mars or something. I'm sure she was probably thinking, *Now why can't you have an imaginary friend like a normal kid?* I wasn't very surprised at her reaction. I mean, it's not every day your eleven-year-old kid just walks up and casually tells you something like that. More likely than not, just as quickly as I'd said it to her was probably just as quickly she forgot all about it, though I certainly never did. Needless to say, from that day 'til this day, I have never told another living soul but kept my little secret tucked away for all these years.

Now don't get me wrong—just because I knew from the start God had a plan for my life doesn't mean that just like that, bada-bing, bada-boom, it was done. Knowing is just the beginning, and truthfully, I wouldn't even say that—that was the beginning to the end. I still had to go through many, many different experiences that would eventually be the "fuel" or the springboard for the task at hand. As encompassed in this book, I had to endure years and years of pain, mistakes, shortcomings, failures, triumphs, frustrations, realizations, revelations, and more in order to have something for God to work with. Refined into something for God to turn around and take the bad and the good and turn it into his gold—"beauty for ashes."

In the years between my youthful revelation and now, I veered off the road, tried many different things, and sometimes even lost sight of what God had told me long ago. There were times I fell from grace because I couldn't see this good plan materializing. I couldn't even see how God would take the mess I was so often enveloped in and transform it into the victory He promised. I told myself I didn't care what I'd thought I'd heard way back when I couldn't do it, therefore I didn't want it.

I often used to feel overwhelmed and think to myself, *Why can't I be like everyone else, going about life in a humdrum way without expectations of grandeur and dreams of fulfilling some master plan that would change my life from mediocre to incredible?* No one else I knew was walking around talking about "God is going to do something great with my life!" None of my friends or family was talking about changing the world or changing lives via some great plan God was working out in them.

Here I was, always sick, deemed and written off by just about every employer I'd ever had as "unemployable" because I couldn't stay out of the hospital long enough to build any kind of consistent attendance on my employment record. With no job and, therefore, no money, I often had to move from one apartment to the next, sometimes ending up having to stay with friends or relatives until I could get back on my feet. Therefore, "Why me?", "I must be crazy," and "What makes me so special?" was all I ever thought about for a long time.

Can you imagine that! How stupid was that—being mad because I had been set aside to be used by God. Of all the outlandish absurdities, to doubt God and MOCK God! All because it wasn't transpiring overnight and I could no longer see the possibility of God's plan unfolding. Which was due mainly to my own negative views and attitude toward myself after so much hardship and a life of many shortcomings, disappointments, and pain. I wasted a lot of years and a lot of possibilities carrying around this negative mind-set for so many years.

The Bible states plainly, "Without FAITH and CONFIDENCE, we cannot receive ANYTHING God is trying to give or impart to us." So it wasn't that God wasn't moving me toward His great plan for my life, but rather, because of my doubt, disbelief, and lack of confidence, I was in no position to even recognize how God was bringing me closer and closer to His plan for my life. Essentially, I was the one holding up my own progress by refusing to cooperate or, most times, to even be willing to receive. So I went around the same mountains over and over and over again for years—WASTING TIME!

All I ever did was complain, "Why God why, when God when?" But I thank God for overlooking my grumbling and complaining and for moving in my life in His time in spite of the fact that I was standing in my own way! If He had not done that, I would not be making the progress that I'm making now, no matter how little it may seem to me. I'd still be lying around in some bed somewhere, wallowing in depression and self-pity. At such a young age, what I believed God would do in my life was one thing; walking it out was a whole other story:

You can believe something, yet your flesh can still prevent you from actually having it happen in your life. I almost allowed—or should I say *helped*—the devil steal God's good plan for my life through *fear* and *disbelief.* Yes, I believed overall what God placed in my heart. Yet when the time came to actually take the STEP of FAITH, to get out of the boat (in order to walk on water) without the doubting, I couldn't. It took heartfelt belief in God's promises so that this great purpose would be fulfilled. I stepped out in FAITH, yet *I couldn't do it right away.* For a long time, I was gripped and paralyzed by fear!

SYDATU HOLDER

BUT GOD WORKED WITH ME. He directed me to good, solid teaching (Joyce Myers Ministries). He got me into the Word and blessed me with wisdom, knowledge, and understanding. He was patient with me. I know—I must have backslid, procrastinated, and had at least a couple of hundred false starts over a period of several years. When it was time to STEP OUT THERE and DO WHAT HE CALLED ME TO DO, I'd tell myself "OK, it's time to do this," and I'd start going at it vigorously for a few days. I'll be studying the Word, praying, positive confessing, asking God for guidance, help, strength and taking time out to write every day. I mean, I'd be on a roll! I'd be so excited I couldn't sleep at night, staying up until four to five o'clock in the morning. All I could think of was working on this grand project, coming up with ideas of what I would write about, what I wanted to say, or rather, what I felt God was speaking about through me. I could hardly wait until the next day so I could get back to it and put down all the things that came to me the night before. I'd set out like I was trying to finish this manuscript in a matter of weeks or a few months! I was focused, or so I thought. Then after about a week or so of this, I'd start slacking off.

By calling me to write this book, God used what He had called me to do—write about my disease and everything associated with it that I talked about so that the world may become knowledgeable about what some people with sickle cell and similar predicaments go through so that someone else with this sickle cell or similar issues won't feel as alone as I did.

Hopefully, this book will help bring about a change in how sickle cell patients are treated by hospitals and health-care administrators. It may heal a lot of the hurts I'd been living with secretly, help to decrease the mental and emotional pain and scars that I've carried around all my life, and honor what God had promised.

There's a passage in the Bible that says God uses the weak and downtrodden, those that the world dismisses and discards as worthless, to do great things for His GLORY.

Isaiah 40:29 He gives strength to the weary and power to the weak and to him who has no might He increases strength causing it to multiply and making it to abound."

2 Corinthians 12:9&10 'He said to me', "My grace is sufficient for you, for my power is made perfect in weakness." That is why, for Christ's sake I delight in insults, in hardship, in persecutions, in difficulties. For when I am weak, then I am strong."

There is no one that fits that bill better than me—I couldn't keep a job, stayed sick, was labeled as physically challenged and limited, and was pitied by many, etc. From the world's point of view, I didn't have a prayer in succeeding in the ladder-climbing, self-serving (you couldn't be the best if you don't have this house or drive that car; you look like a loser) society we live in.

Of course, your chances of getting up the ladder greatly improve if you're a blond-haired, blue-eyed Ivy League school graduate and a popular social butterfly. Someone like me isn't supposed to go on and do something incredible and great. But thank God it isn't about what I can or can't do, what skills or abilities I do or don't have, what family background or life situation I did or did not come from.

It's about what God can do and the strength, courage, and anointing that I have through Him to fulfill the purpose He set for my life, even before the creation of this world, before I was even conceived.

It's all about His righteousness in me to do and be all that He has called me to.

SYDATU HOLDER

As You Believe

I want to believe that my future holds promise
I want to believe that the constant nightmares
Of failures that plague my soul are not my destiny
I want to believe in myself, be confident
That I am the whosoever of God's promises
I want to believe that my dreams will come true
In spite of myself and my faithless will
But it's hard
It's hard to see the garden of flowers awaiting
Beyond the tall oaks of the heartbreak of mediocrity
Yes, mediocrity is heartbreaking when you're anointed
With purpose and divine destiny
That is the noose around my neck that's slowly suffocating me
How can you be dead when you're alive
It's not hard
This world is saturated with the living dead
Only I wasn't supposed to be one of them
I'm destined for greatness
That's what I've been told, and
That's what I desperately want to believe
That's what I'd believe
If only I could get out of my own way
My reflection in the mirror telling me
That's the source of my pain
I want to believe I've got what it takes
But where is it—vacationing?
I want to believe
I don't have to be buried with or by my mistakes
I want to believe
That I can get out of this coffin
Let the Caretaker hold my baggage
I want to believe that my tear-stained pillow
Will save me from myself, my life
He and His legion of angels
He said ask, so I asked
He said seek, and I sought

He said knock, and I began banging and pounding
And then He said
It will be given to you,
You will find it, and it will be opened onto you
But then, I stopped
Just like that, I stopped; right in the middle of the road
I fell from grace and stopped believing
I stopped believing in mountain moving, mustard seeds
So be it
(Unto you that is) as you believe
Unto me—I want to believe that
Especially in the still of night
When I'm consumed by darkness
When fear sets upon me, paralyzing
And diminishing all those promises
Replacing them with waves of nausea,
Sleepless nights and depressed days
Carrying around sacks full of pain,
Foreboding regret and hopelessness
In a trance I can't escape
Wishing time would fall away
That my last day was yesterday
So much for "Carpe diem" (seize the day)
I'm sure even He's tired of me
I want to believe, I have to believe
Now, if only I would get out of my own way.

Phoenix, April 3, 2006

SYDATU HOLDER

She Got to Do All the Things She Wanted Before She Died

My cousin died today
Breast cancer—complications, I'm told
She was all of thirty-six years old
My sister said, "At least she got to do all the things she wanted to
do,
Or at least she tried"

She got to do all the things she wanted to do
Or at least she tried
I guess she knew then what we know now
And being diagnosed made her decide
Or at least must've helped make up her mind
'Cause she knew then what we know now . . . she was gonna die

Who'd have believed then
What we've just learned now
This day would come sooner than later, surely not one of us
She was much too young
Though it seems all the greats do die young
My dad, then her dad
And countless others among them
Not seeing her vibrant spirit or hear her laugh
A laugh that was contagious, that even if you wanted to be mad,
you'd have to smile

Baby Girl

Not many people out there you can put your trust in
More times than not, there won't be any

A man will do only what you allow him to
Your body is your temple, so be careful what you do
Always be true to yourself, never be afraid to just be you

Support yourself throughout your life
Cause there will be those like, "What's yours is mine and what's
mine is mine"
So you gotta be prepared when it comes that time
Or you'll end up some clown's concubine

You would tell me if I want the world, go out and get it
Never settle for less 'cause in this world, second best don't cut it
If the sky's the limit, I'm gonna reach for the stars

Being hardheaded, I learned a lot of hard lessons
Moms would say, "A hard head leaves a soft behind," but I still
don't wanna listen
If I knew then half of what I know now, I'd have paid attention

With everything she taught me and what I learned on my own
I'ma tell you, "Watch your step, baby girl, you'll have plenty of
time to be grown"

SYDATU HOLDER

Lightning Source UK Ltd.
Milton Keynes UK
UKOW04f0953030917
308466UK00001B/26/P